FAS...
CELEBRITY
FACTS

FASCINATING CELEBRITY FACTS

HANNAH WARNER

TED SMART

First published in 2003 by
Virgin Books Ltd
Thames Wharf Studios
Rainville Road
London
W6 9HA

A catalogue record for this book is available from
the British Library.

This edition produced for The Book People Ltd
Hall Wood Avenue, Haydock, St Helens, WA11 9UL

ISBN 0 7535 0852 4

Designed and typeset by Undertow Design
Printed and bound in Great Britain by
Clays Ltd, St Ives PLC

CONTENTS

ACKNOWLEDGEMENTS

Thanks to John and Pat Cleveland, who always let me watch *Coronation Street* before sending me to bed, and to Charlotte Cleveland, who always fills me in if I miss any reality television shows.

Thank you to Barbara Phelan for liking my idea for the book and for agreeing to publish it, and to Clair Holden and Al Booth for providing me with some really good facts.

Finally, thanks to Tim Warner, who has never really been interested in celebrities but who has helped me so much – from making cups of tea to correcting my spelling and making me smile again when I was in a bad mood.

★ ★ ★ ★ ★ ★ ★ ★ ★ ★ ★ ★ ★ ★
INTRODUCTION
★ ★ ★ ★ ★ ★ ★ ★ ★ ★ ★ ★ ★ ★

I have always been interested in the lives of the rich and famous. From the time I could read I can remember being excited about visiting my Auntie Sandra's house because she had *all* the tabloid newspapers on a Sunday. Once there I would barely utter a word as I absorbed all the information I could about the apparently exciting and glamorous lives of those I saw on the television and listened to on the radio, and would pass on what I had learned to anyone who would listen.

My interest in the world of show business continued, and I eventually got to work as producer on BBC Radio 2's successful *Steve Wright in the Afternoon* show. As part of my job I had to research the lives of the famous people who came on the show. From Paul McCartney and Kylie Minogue to Anne Robinson and Nicolas Cage, I was actually being paid to indulge in my hobby of reading autobiographies and news cuttings, in order to find out more about them.

While I worked, I would often annoy the other members of the programme team who worked in the office with trivial facts I had discovered, and it was this that led me to come up with the idea for this book.

I have often wondered why we as a nation have become so obsessed with celebrity, and have come to the conclusion that it is all to do with neighbours, and I don't mean the TV programme.

Years ago everyone knew who their neighbours were, and would frequently twitch at their net curtains in the front room, having a peek at what was going on in the lives of those who lived down their street. It was a case of watching from the outside without actually getting involved, something to gossip about and pass comment on with family, friends and other neighbours. Nowadays many of us no longer know our neighbours but, through the proliferation of celebrity magazines and chat shows, as well as the tabloids, we can take a peek at the lives of those we see on the television, people we talk about with the same familiarity as we once spoke about those who lived over the road. We feel we know them, even though we don't see what goes on behind their front door. We chat about everything from what they wear and how they look, to who they are going out with and whether the relationship will last.

This book hopefully fills in some of the gaps in your knowledge of the famous, and will allow you to show off in front of your friends next time you talk about celebrities at the pub or over a cup of coffee. I hope you enjoy it.

SCHOOL DAYS

They are meant to be the best days of our lives, but for some celebrities they are times they would rather not be reminded about.

This section features a mixture of facts about those famous people who shone at school, those who teachers prefer to forget, and others whose early days were an indication of what was to come in later life.

★ One of David Bowie's eyes changed colour after a compass-stabbing incident at school.

★ Actors Robin Williams and Tom Cruise were both voted the pupil 'Least Likely to Succeed' while at school.

★ When she was eight, *Countdown's* Carol Vorderman's teacher wrote in her school report that 'Carol has a masterly hold over mathematical computation which should prove profitable later on'.

★ *EastEnders'* Ian Beale, actor Adam Woodyatt, was in the same class at school as England cricket captain Nasser Hussain.

★ Actor Hugh Grant once appeared in the children's television school quiz *Top of the Form*.

★ Writer and broadcaster Gyles Brandreth enjoyed travelling on the tube so much while he was at school that he used to do his exam revision on the Central Line, stopping for a cup of tea every time he reached Paddington station.

★ *Pearl Harbor* actress Kate Beckinsale won the WH Smith Young Writers' Competition for both her fiction and poetry while studying at school.

★ Actor Jack Nicholson was in detention every day for one whole school year.

★ Prime Minister Tony Blair once ran away from his school. One housemaster called him 'the most difficult boy I ever had to deal with'.

★ Former 'It Girl' Tamara Beckwith left Cheltenham Ladies' College 'by mutual consent', after turning up at the school with a punk hairstyle.

★ Oscar-winning actor Michael Caine was known as 'snake eyes' at school.

★ Television presenter Judy Finnegan had elocution lessons while at Manchester High School to get rid of her strong Mancunian accent.

★ Oscar winner Nicolas Cage was expelled from school for putting grasshoppers in the egg salad during a school picnic.

★ Television cook Nigella Lawson failed her eleven-plus by refusing to take a maths paper.

★ MP John Prescott also failed his eleven-plus, and left school without any qualifications.

★ When writer Roald Dahl was fifteen, his English teacher wrote in his report that he seemed 'incapable of marshalling his thoughts on paper'.

★ Actor and comedian Billy Crystal was voted 'Best Personality of the Class of '65' at school.

★ *Prime Suspect* actress Helen Mirren upset nuns at her convent school when she set up a darts stall at a local fairground.

★ Comedian and actor Stephen Fry had passed nine O levels by the time he was thirteen.

★ Madonna was given the roles of both School-hall monitor and Campfire Girl while at school.

★ David Jason won awards for gymnastics at school.

★ Newsreader Jon Snow was thrown out of Liverpool University for leading an anti-apartheid demonstration.

★ In high school, singer Mariah Carey's nickname was 'Mirage' because she would often be absent from classes.

★ Liam Neeson, Sir Ian McKellen and Ian Hislop were all head boys of their schools.

★ *X-Files* actor David Duchovny had an accident while playing basketball in high school, which damaged his right eye. He is said to use dye to keep the colour right and to keep the pupil from dilating too much.

★ Hellraising Pogues' front man Shane MacGowan attended Westminster Public School.

★ James Dean shone in the public debating arena while at school. He was the 1949 Iowa champion of the National Forensic League.

★ Hollywood director Steven Spielberg was nicknamed 'The Retard' at school.

★ When presenter Nadia Sawalha was thirteen, she emptied a fire extinguisher all over her headmistress's office, while she was in the room. Sawalha was suspended.

★ While attending the Sylvia Young Stage School, presenter and musical star Denise van Outen used to sleep with her hair in rollers.

★ When Richard Branson left school, his headmaster told him, 'I predict you will either go to prison or become a millionaire'.

★ *Bad Girls* actress Nicole Faraday, who played murderer Snowball Merriman, was expelled from school when she was fifteen, after making a fake bomb out of an alarm clock, Blu-Tack and old telephone wires. She thought the stunt would be taken as a joke, but the bomb squad were called and were preparing to do a controlled explosion when Faraday finally owned up. She received a juvenile warning from police.

★ Model Jerry Hall won a science scholarship at school.

★ When American talk-show host Jay Leno was in fifth grade, his teacher wrote on his report card: 'If Jay spent as much time studying as he does trying to be a comedian, he'd be a big star.'

★ *Absolutely Fabulous* actress Joanna Lumley was sacked as a prefect at school after being caught smoking.

★ Mo Mowlam, Kate Winslet, JK Rowling and Sarah Ferguson were all head girls at school.

★ Jeremy Paxman's school housemaster said of the *Newsnight* presenter, 'His stubbornness is in his nature, and could be an asset when directed to sound ends.'

★ Long before he was drinking Chianti, *Silence of the Lambs* actor Anthony Hopkins used to impress his classmates by drinking ink.

★ When Anne Robinson left school, her maths teacher told her she would 'never make anything of herself'.

★ Aged thirteen, actress Helena Bonham Carter spent her £25 school poetry prize on buying space in *Spotlight*, the theatrical casting directory.

★ The man behind the distinctive voice of Victor Meldrew, actor Richard Wilson, had his acting ambitions laughed at by his school drama teacher who told him, 'Don't be silly boy, you can't speak properly.'

★ As a schoolboy Rory Bremner used to amuse his classmates with his impression of *The Good Life*'s Penelope Keith.

★ Pop star Nicole Appleton was suspended from school for stealing Wotsits from a fellow pupil. She got caught because her fingers were orange.

★ Nicole also used to go to sleep in her school uniform, so she could enjoy more time in bed in the morning.

★ *Ground Force* presenter Charlie Dimmock was nicknamed 'Ginger Nut' and 'Duracell' at school, because of her distinctive red hair.

★ *Dirty Dancing* star Patrick Swayze was teased at school because he liked to dance.

★ Monica Lewinsky's classmates voted her 'The Girl Most Likely to Get Her Name in Lights'.

★ Nicole Kidman was called 'The Stork' at school, because of her height. She was 5ft 9in by the time she was thirteen years old.

★ Sigourney Weaver was another tall school pupil. She was 6ft tall by the time she was twelve years old.

★ Presenter Davina McCall and cook Nigella Lawson both attended the same school – Godolphin and Latymer – in London.

★ Comedian Frank Skinner was expelled from school when he was sixteen.

★ One teacher once wrote of *Pop Idol's* Will Young, 'My heart sank when I learned that William was in my class.'

★ Actor Michael Douglas was nicknamed 'Little Spartacus' at school, after his father Kirk's epic role in the film of the same name.

★ *Watchdog* presenter Nicky Campbell was once suspended from school after being caught with a packet of cigarettes in his blazer pocket.

★ *Who Wants to be a Millionaire?* host Chris Tarrant was caned at school, after being caught skiving with girls from the neighbouring boarding school.

★ Actress Michelle Pfeiffer was bullied at school because of her big lips.

★ Singer and *Blind Date* presenter Cilla Black's last school report read 'Priscilla is suitable for office work'.

★ Bob Hoskins once embarrassed his headmaster while at school by putting a condom in his Bible.

★ American President John F Kennedy was voted the pupil 'Most Likely to Succeed', even thought he graduated 64th out of his high-school class of 112.

★ Celine Dion was known as 'Vampire Queen' in high school because of her sharp canine teeth.

★ *Friends* star David Schwimmer attended Beverly Hills High School, which was the inspiration for the television series *Beverly Hills 90210*.

★ Robin and Maurice Gibb from The Bee Gees left school at thirteen.

★ Les Dennis and Sir Paul McCartney both attended Stockton Wood Primary School.

★ Sylvester Stallone was voted 'Most Likely to end up in the Electric Chair' by his schoolmates. He was expelled from fourteen schools in eleven years.

★ *Bargain Hunt's* David Dickinson was 'king of the conkers' at school.

★ Despite a reputation as being something of an airhead, Tara Palmer-Tomkinson left school with ten O levels and three A levels.

★ Meanwhile former Prime Minister John Major left school

without obtaining any qualifications.

★ *EastEnders*' Wendy Richard was knocked over by a car on her first day at stage school. She needed 32 stitches.

★ Film star Robert de Niro was nicknamed 'Bobby Milk' while he was at school, because of his complexion.

★ Television presenter Dale Winton was regularly caned at his boarding school, for talking after the lights were out.

★ Judy Finnegan used to avoid taking part in games lessons at school by creeping through the school fence into her parents' garden, which backed on to the school grounds. She and her friend would spend the lessons playing records and drinking coffee.

★ Halle Berry was elected 'Prom Queen' at high school, but nearly lost her crown after being accused of ballot-box stuffing.

★ The head teacher of Lancaster Road Junior School said of comedian Eric Morecambe, 'this boy will never get anywhere in life'.

★ During the 1980s, Victoria Beckham started a trend at her school of wearing two pairs of socks at the same time, giving the impression of wearing socks and legwarmers.

★ *Four Weddings and a Funeral* actress Kristin Scott Thomas left the Central School of Speech and Drama after one of the teachers informed her that she would never make it as an actress.

★ *Reservoir Dogs* star Harvey Keitel was expelled from school for repeated truancy.

★ While she was at primary school, former Catatonia singer Cerys Matthews was nicknamed 'The Dentist' because she used to extract her classmates milk teeth.

★ Russell Crowe lost his front tooth playing rugby at school when he was ten. He didn't get it fixed until the director of *The*

Crossing insisted he do so.

★ Television trickster Jeremy Beadle was expelled from school for hanging a pair of trousers, 'among other things', from a flagpole.

★ *Speed* star Sandra Bullock was voted 'Most Likely to Brighten up Your Day' while at school.

★ Tony Blair was once mistaken for a burglar while at school, and arrested.

★ Harrison Ford was bullied at school because he liked to hang around with girls.

★ While at primary school, Nicole Kidman pretended that she was a witch for two years. She was so convincing that most of her classmates believed her.

★ Former MP Mo Mowlam regarded school fire practices as a waste of time, because the teachers always knew they were going to take place, so she once set the fire alarm off herself to test the system.

★ Television presenter Zoe Ball was called 'FA Cup' when she was at school because of the shape of her ears.

★ *Newsnights'* Jeremy Paxman blames his aggression on being bullied as a pupil at school.

★ Meg Ryan was voted 'The Cutest Girl in Class' at school.

★ Record-breaking yachtswoman Ellen McArthur saved her school dinner money for three years to help buy her own boat: an eight-foot dinghy named *Threep'ny Bit*.

★ Keanu Reeves was known as 'The Wall' at school. Some have said this is because of his talent for hockey, while others have put it down to his blank stare.

★ ★ ★ ★ ★ ★ ★ ★ ★ ★ ★ ★ ★ ★ ★ ★ ★
CELEBRITY GRADUATES
★ ★ ★ ★ ★ ★ ★ ★ ★ ★ ★ ★ ★ ★ ★ ★ ★

Some celebrities are not known for their intelligence. *Big Brother 3's* Jade Goody thought that Rio de Janeiro was a person and Portugal was in Spain, while Christine Hamilton cried with shame when she and husband Neil won only £100 on *Who Wants to be a Millionaire?* after not knowing whether 'Red Red Wine' or 'Black Black Coffee' was a hit for UB40.

It's good to know, then, that some famous people have a degree of knowledge.

Cate Blanchett – Economics and Fine Arts

John Cleese – Law

Richard Blackwood – Business Studies

Glenn Close – Anthropology

Hugh Grant – English Literature

Jonathan Ross – East European Modern History

Brian May – Physics

Hugh Hefner – Psychology

Sanjeev Bhaskar – Marketing

Lucy Liu – Asian Languages and Culture

Rowan Atkinson – Electrical Engineering

Paul Newman – Economics and Dramatics

Brooke Shields – French Literature

Sandra Bullock – Drama

Hugh Bonneville – Theology

Kate Beckinsale – Russian and French

Julie Walters – Nursing

Lisa Kudrow – Biology

Rory Bremner – French and German

Bruce Lee – Philosophy

Brad Pitt – Journalism

Carol Vorderman – Engineering

Rick Stein – English

Alec Baldwin – Political Science

★ BEFORE THEY WERE FAMOUS

Not all stars of stage and screen find fame overnight. For every Michael Jackson, Charlotte Church and Britney Spears who enjoyed life in front of the camera from an early age, there are many more who struggled to get not just their first starring role, but any role at all! It's good to know that, just like us, they have had some not so glamorous jobs.

★ Before finding fame as 007, actor Sean Connery once worked as a coffin polisher.

★ Also at the undertakers – *Sister Act* star Whoopi Goldberg, who used to apply make-up to corpses in funeral parlours.

★ Meanwhile singer Rod Stewart and record producer Pete Waterman have both earned a crust as gravediggers.

★ During her modelling days, *Changing Rooms* presenter Carol Smillie once posed as 'Holly Wholemeal' for a Flour Advisory Board promotion.

★ Long before she was seen pouring coffee in Central Perk, *Friends* star Jennifer Aniston worked as a waitress.

★ Disgraced former Tory MP Jeffrey Archer was once a deck chair attendant.

★ *Big Brother* presenter Davina McCall's first job was as a singing waitress in Paris.

★ Sharleen Spiteri, lead singer of the band Texas, used to earn a living as a hairdresser, as did Hollywood actor Danny de Vito,

60s model Twiggy and Delia Smith.

★ Harrison Ford was working as a carpenter when he was given the role of Han Solo. Ford had been struggling to find acting work and so was repairing the porch entrance at the Goldwyn studios when George Lucas asked him to fill in at a *Star Wars* audition. Harrison read so well for the part that Lucas ended up casting him in the film.

★ Before he was enjoying the *Last of the Summer Wine*, Peter Sallis was a Co-op manager.

★ Many years before he bit the head off a bat and moved to Los Angeles, Ozzy Osbourne worked as a labourer in a slaughterhouse.

★ As a teenager, Andie MacDowell worked at McDonald's and Pizza Hut.

★ Singer Elvis Costello is said to have to wear glasses as a result of straining his eyes while working as a computer programmer.

★ One of *Prime Suspect* actress Helen Mirren's first roles was at an amusement park in Southend. She was a 'blagger', which entailed attracting people on to the rides.

★ Television presenter Graham Norton spent one university summer holiday busking outside the Pompidou centre in Paris. He would walk up behind people and mimic them, copying their walk and their mannerisms.

★ As a young man, Hollywood director Steven Spielberg once spent a summer whitewashing fruit trees.

★ William Roache, *Coronation Street*'s Ken Barlow, served as an army captain in his twenties.

★ Fellow *Coronation Street* star Johnny Briggs, who plays Mike Baldwin, used to perform as an opera singer.

FASCINATING CELEBRITY FACTS

★ Before becoming the 'Material Girl', Madonna spent time as a lifeguard.

★ While struggling as a young actor, James Bond actor Pierce Brosnan earned extra money by driving minicabs and bought his clothes from charity shops.

★ *The Usual Suspects* star Gabriel Byrne was an archaeologist, a schoolteacher, a short-order cook, and a bullfighter before he was an actor.

★ A young Barbara Windsor was said to have used her charms to encourage men to buy shoes for their wives and girlfriends when she worked in a shoe shop.

★ Hollywood heart-throb Brad Pitt has earned money driving limousines and delivering fridges.

★ Dame Shirley Bassey's first job was packing enamel chamber pots. She claims she used to write her name on them and got replies from all over the world.

★ *Sharpe* star Sean Bean once worked for Sheffield council as a snow clearer.

★ Before appearing on cinema screens, Hollywood tough guy Mickey Rourke worked in a cinema as an usher. He was sacked from his job after getting into a brawl with one of his workmates.

★ *T4* presenter Vernon Kay went from working as a cleaner to cruising down the catwalks, after being spotted by a model agency scout at a 'Clothes Show Live' exhibition.

★ While struggling as an actor, a young Rupert Everett wrote a book – it was called *Hello Darling, Are You Working?*

★ Long before she ever worked in the launderette, *EastEnders*' Wendy Richard worked in the fashion department of Fortnum and Mason.

★ *Animal Hospital* presenter Rolf Harris's early career did not involve the delivery of animals, but the delivery of letters – he was a postman.

★ Before she embarked on a *Titanic* acting career, Kate Winslet served behind the counter at a London deli.

★ *American Beauty* star Kevin Spacey used to be a stand-up comic before moving into serious acting.

★ *Ally McBeal* star Calista Flockhart used to work as an aerobics instructor before getting her big break.

★ Before he hit the big time with Culture Club, DJ Boy George worked at a supermarket. He was sacked from his job for wearing the store's carrier bags. The supermarket reportedly described his appearance as 'disturbing'.

★ As well as being the tough guy on screen, *Rambo* and *Rocky* star Sylvester Stallone proved his bravery off screen when he was employed as a lion-cage cleaner.

★ *Trigger Happy TV* star Dom Joly worked in Prague for nine months as a diplomat for the European Commission.

★ Before becoming the star of the *Carry On* series of films, Sid James worked as a hairdresser, dance instructor, roller skater and coal heaver.

★ Oscar winner Julie Walters originally trained as a nurse.

★ Before he became the nation's *Pop Idol*, Will Young spent university holidays working as a gardener.

★ Eurythmics singer Annie Lennox once had a far less glamorous occupation – she used to be a fish filleter.

★ *Only Fools and Horses* star David Jason was 26 before he got into acting. Prior to that he worked as an electrician.

★ Comedian Julian Clary's first job after university was with

British Gas – doing the photocopying. He also worked as a gay Tarzan kissagram.

★ Elvis Presley was sacked from his job at the Precision Tool Company in Memphis when his bosses discovered he was actually fifteen years old, and therefore too young to work there.

★ Bob Geldof worked as a hot-dog salesman as well as an assistant in an abattoir before finding fame as lead singer of the Boomtown Rats and later as the organiser of Live Aid.

★ Before joining Take That, singer Robbie Williams worked as a double-glazing salesman. He has claimed that he annoyed his employers by telling the customers how bad the glazing was.

★ *EastEnder* Shane Richie earned money cleaning up after donkeys and running the donkey derby while he was in his teens.

★ Magician Paul Daniels used to run a grocer's shop.

★ Rolling Stone Mick Jagger was once a porter in a psychiatric hospital.

★ Comedian Jasper Carrott's first job after leaving school at sixteen was as a denture paste salesman.

★ Des Lynam wasn't always a sports presenter. For twenty years he worked as an insurance salesman.

★ The first job of I'm a *Celebrity … Get Me Out of Here* winner Tony Blackburn was as a singer and guitarist with the Ian Ralfini Orchestra at Bournemouth Pavilion.

★ Actress Gillian Taylforth was a legal secretary for nine years before she joined *EastEnders*, using her holidays to do any acting jobs that came up.

★ *Speed* and *Matrix* star Keanu Reeves once managed a pasta shop in Toronto.

★ Hugh Grant gained valuable photo-shoot experience before

hitting the big time with *Four Weddings and a Funeral* – he used to model for teen magazines.

★ *Have I Got News for You* panellist Paul Merton spent three years working at Tooting Employment Exchange.

★ Ulrika Jonsson, Caroline Aherne and Mystic Meg have all worked as secretaries.

★ Jewellery wearing DJ Jimmy Saville was a Yorkshire coal miner in his youth.

★ David Beckham once earned £2 a night collecting empty glasses at Walthamstow dog track.

★ *Stars in Your Eyes* presenter Matthew Kelly's first job was as a bingo caller, as was *Cold Feet* star James Nesbitt and Westlife's Bryan McFadden.

★ Terry Wogan was a Bank of Ireland cashier for five years before moving to a Dublin radio station, where he read out cattle market reports.

★ Fellow Radio 2 presenter Steve Wright worked for British Telecom .

★ As well as his bingo job, Westlife's Bryan McFadden used to keep the peace at his local burger bar, where he worked as a security guard.

ON THE ROAD TO FAME

Some stars of stage and screen have spent their whole life harbouring an ambition to perform. However, very few get to top the bill before they have served their time in less prominent roles. Even former Bond actor Roger Moore had to spend time in front of the camera modelling knitwear before he was given his licence to kill.

★ Jude Law made an early television appearance in the 90s playing Nathan Thompson in the ITV afternoon soap opera *Families*.

★ One of Barbara Windsor's earliest appearances was as an unnamed schoolgirl in the 1954 film, *The Belles of St Trinian's*.

★ Before appearing on screen as an actress, Tamzin Outhwaite appeared as a presenter on the BBC2 youth show *No Limits*, where she was known as 'Tammi' Outhwaite.

★ *Just Good Friends* actor Paul Nicholas had a musical start to his career – he was the pianist in Screaming Lord Sutch's band.

★ Elton John began his musical career playing the piano in a pub in Pinner in Middlesex. He earned 50p a night.

★ Long before he was entertaining the audience with his own shows, Michael Barrymore was the warm-up man for the Larry Grayson version of *The Generation Game*.

★ *The Fast Show's* Paul Whitehouse got into comedy when he and *Fast Show* co-star Charlie Higson were employed by Harry Enfield to write for his show. Until that point Paul had been working as a plasterer after dropping out of the University of East Anglia.

★ *Hollyoaks* actor Nick Pickard, who plays Tony Hutchinson, made an early big-screen appearance in the Steven Spielberg film *Empire of the Sun*.

★ Martin Kemp once appeared in a film for children's TV show *Jackanory*.

★ Before he appeared in front of the camera, American comic actor Steve Martin used to write for many other performers including Dick van Dyke, singer John Denver, and Sonny and Cher.

★ INXS front man Michael Hutchence's first recording was a version of 'Jingle Bells', which was used in a talking doll.

★ Television presenter Alice Beer's first job was as a secretary on the BBC consumer programme *That's Life*.

★ Before he was 'going wild in the aisles' on *Supermarket Sweep*, television presenter Dale Winton began his career as a DJ on United Biscuits Industrial Radio.

★ BBC Radio 1 presenter Jo Whiley used to work as a band booker on *The Word*.

★ Jennifer Lopez appeared in the video for the Janet Jackson single 'That's the Way Love Goes'.

★ Mike Reid may now be known for playing Frank Butcher in *EastEnders*, but his first TV acting role was as a soldier in *Dr Who* in 1966.

★ *EastEnders*' Elaine Lordan, who plays Lynne Slater, appeared alongside fellow *EastEnder* Todd Carty (Mark Fowler) in the children's series *Tucker's Luck*.

★ *EastEnders*' Perry Fenwick, a.k.a. Billy Mitchell, also made an early appearance in *Tucker's Luck*. He played the drummer in Tucker's band.

★ Noel Gallagher's first step on the rock'n'roll ladder was as a roadie for the Inspiral Carpets in 1988, after a chance meeting with them at a Stone Roses concert.

★ Former Spice Girl Geri Halliwell once worked as a hostess on a Turkish game show.

★ Before finding fame in front of the cameras as a comedian and quiz-show host, Bob Monkhouse wrote material for Bob Hope, Frank Sinatra, Dean Martin and Jerry Lewis.

★ Jack Nicholson also worked behind the camera on the road to fame. He used to be a messenger boy for a film company's cartoon department, and at one time answered fan mail for *Tom and Jerry*.

★ Television and radio presenter Chris Evans's first job in radio was as Timmy Mallett's teaboy. He also worked as a Tarzan-o-gram and a forklift truck driver.

★ Television presenters Fiona Phillips and Anthea Turner, and Radio 1 chart-show host Wes Butter all gained early broadcasting experience by reading the traffic reports on local radio stations.

★ Before he wowed the world as Robin Hood, Kevin Costner appeared in a soft-porn film called *Sizzle Beach, USA*.

★ One of Jamie Theakston's first television appearances was as a nineteen-year-old, parading along the catwalk of a *Clothes Show* modelling competition.

★ Before becoming one third of Atomic Kitten, Kerry McFadden performed on stage as a lap dancer.

★ Many years before he wowed the world as Austin Powers, Mike Myers was a presenter on TV-AM's children's programme *The Wide Awake Club*.

★ Kurt Russell made an early film appearance in the Elvis Presley film *It Happened at the World's Fair*, where he was billed as 'boy who kicks Elvis'. Years later Russell was to take on the role of The King in the film *Elvis*.

★ Long before he teamed up with Declan Donnelly on the set of *Byker Grove*, Ant McPartlin was a presenter on the children's programme *Why Don't You?*

★ Hollywood actress Goldie Hawn worked as a can-can dancer and a go-go dancer before finding fame and fortune in films.

★ Before becoming well known as *Emmerdale*'s favourite schizophrenic lesbian Zoe Tate, actress Leah Bracknell performed alongside comedy duo Cannon and Ball.

★ Supermodel Naomi Campbell had a role as an extra in *Grange Hill* before she forged a career on the catwalk. Other famous people to don the uniform were *ER*'s Alex Kingston, who played a school bully, as well as *EastEnders*' Letitia Dean and Patsy Palmer.

★ *Birds of a Feather* star Pauline Quirke had a role in *Dixon of Dock Green* when she was only nine, and became Britain's youngest television presenter with her show *Pauline's Quirks*.

★ Actress Amanda Holden made an early television appearance as a contestant on *Blind Date* in 1990, when she was nineteen. *GMTV* presenter Jenni Falconer also appeared alongside Cilla Black in 1994, when she chose a twenty-stone chip-shop owner as her date.

★ *The Wright Stuff* presenter Matthew Wright made it on to the screen at the age of fourteen when he starred in *Big Wheels and Sailors* for the Children's Film Foundation.

★ Melinda Messenger got her big break when she fronted an advertising campaign for a double-glazing company. The company's advertising slogan was 'Class behind glass'.

★ *EastEnders*' evil Trevor Morgan, actor Alex Ferns, was a household name in South Africa before arriving in Albert Square – he appeared as a gay hairdresser in the country's biggest soap, *Generations*.

★ Christopher Parker, *EastEnders*' Spencer Moon, was a stunt double in the Harry Potter films.

★ Before he was telling thousands of screaming girls to 'All Rise', Blue's Lee Ryan appeared in front of the camera as an actor. He appeared in an episode of *Holby City*, playing a concussed teenager.

★ Actor Paul Usher, formerly *Brookside*'s bad boy Barry Grant, and now PC Des Taviner in *The Bill*, got his television break in an episode of the long-running police series *Z Cars* when he was sixteen.

★ *Smack the Pony*'s Fiona Allen's first television role was in a government anti-drink-driving advert, where she played a car-crash victim.

★ Corrie's Curly Watts, actor Kevin Kennedy, made his television debut as a team helper on *Cheggers Plays Pop*.

★ Singer Sophie Ellis-Bextor made some early television appearances on *Blue Peter*, while her mum Janet Ellis was a presenter on the show – she was seen once modelling a 'snood' and another time modelling a dress made out of dustbin liners with little bows on it.

★ *Sex and the City* actress Kristin Davis appeared in US teen drama *Melrose Place* before heading to New York. She was written out of the show after only one year because her character, Brooke, was disliked so much.

★ Charlotte Church first appeared on television aged eleven, when she introduced her aunt Caroline, who was one of the contestants on Jonathan Ross's *Big, Big Talent Show*, and was invited to sing a few words. However, she had been heard the previous week, when she entered a competition on *This Morning* for talented children, and sang down the phone to Richard and Judy.

★ Ruby Wax worked as a scriptwriter on the 80s comedy sketch show *Not the Nine O'Clock News*.

★ Before he was President of the United States, and even before he was an actor, Ronald Reagan was a sports broadcaster. It has been said that he used to pretend he was commentating on the Chicago Cubs games from the club's ground, when he was actually sitting in the studios of his radio station, receiving reports on the game via telegraph.

★ Hollywood star Samuel L Jackson spent two years as Bill Cosby's stand-in during filming of *The Cosby Show*.

★ *Down to Earth* star Ian Kelsey's first screen appearance was in an early episode of *Men Behaving Badly*, where he was seen performing as a karaoke singer.

★ Impressionist Rory Bremner made his first television appearance on *The Tube* in 1984.

★ Before she was performing on stages around the globe, Andrea Corr appeared as Jimmy Rabbitte's sister in the 1991 Alan Parker film *The Commitments*.

★ Long before he received a Best Comedy Actor award at the British Comedy Awards, *Marion and Geoff* star Rob Brydon presented a show on a shopping channel.

COMMERCIAL CELEBRITIES

The stars have always been keen to appear in adverts. For some it was a first opportunity to be seen on television, a chance to be spotted by producers who would sign them up for Hollywood movies. For already established artists, however, it has been the chance to earn a lot of money for very little work! Indeed actress Jane Horrocks has nicknamed her house 'Tesco Towers', as it was paid for with the money she received for appearing in a series of commercials for the supermarket.

★ Stage-school classmates Emma Bunton and *Emmerdale* actress Sheree Murphy, who plays barmaid Tricia Dingle, starred together in an advert before embarking on their separate roads to fame. The pair played bridesmaids who were catapulted onto a human wedding cake in a commercial for the Halifax Building Society.

★ Before joining *EastEnders*, actress Kasey Ainsworth appeared in a cinema advert for the Mini Cooper. It was banned for being too risqué.

★ Fellow *EastEnder* Lucy Speed, who plays Natalie Evans, made early television appearances in adverts for Sun-Pat peanut butter, gas, paint and soup.

★ In the late 1980s Madonna was paid £3 million to advertise Pepsi. The ad was short-lived however, when the company was forced to drop it following protests that the video to her song 'Like a Prayer', which was heard on the advert, was blasphemous.

★ Jonathan Ross once advertised Harp lager, but his contract was cut short because it was feared that he might attract under-age drinkers.

★ Actress Maureen Lipman made 55 adverts for British Telecom over five years, yet only 35 of them were ever broadcast.

★ Billie Piper found fame as a singer after appearing as the face of a *Smash Hits* advert in August 1997.

★ Hollywood actress Jodie Foster made her screen debut as a three-year-old in an advert for Coppertone suntan lotion. Her brother Buddy was originally up for the advert, and Jodie had only been taken along as she was too young to be left in the house on her own. The advert involved her having her pants pulled down by a dog. Over the next five years, Foster appeared in 56 more commercials.

★ Amanda Holden once appeared in an advert for Haven Holidays. Their mascot was a tiger and Amanda had to sit by him pretending she was having fun.

★ Holden's *Cutting It* co-star Sarah Parish also got her television break by appearing in an advert – for Boddington's bitter. Unfortunately, following the advert many television executives believed she came from the north, as opposed to her native Somerset.

★ Television and radio presenter Terry Wogan promoted the Playtex 'Living Bra' in the 1970s. The bra came with a seven-minute disc of exercises.

★ Cilla Black once put the 'oo' in Typhoo. She appeared in a commercial dressed as a waitress.

★ In the late 80s *Minder* star George Cole played a character not unlike Arthur Daley in an advert for the Leeds Permanent Building Society. Rival building societies complained to the advertising watchdog.

★ *Friends* star Courtney Cox made television history in America when she starred in a Tampax advert, by uttering the then-taboo word 'period' when referring to her menstrual cycle.

★ Lynda Bellingham made her first appearance as head of the Oxo family in 1983. The series of adverts ran for almost twenty years.

★ *High Fidelity* star John Cusack was appearing in adverts for Heinz and MacDonald's before he was a teenager.

★ Comedian Jack Dee used to front the advertising campaign for John Smith's bitter, despite being teetotal himself.

★ Meanwhile American golfer Tiger Woods was paid £700,000 a year to endorse the Nike Tour Accuracy brand of golf ball – even though he later admitted that he did not use the ball himself.

★ Carol Vorderman's contract with *Tomorrow's World* was terminated in May 1995 after her appearance in an advert for Ariel washing powder.

★ And gardener Percy Thrower was replaced as host of the BBC's *Gardener's World* programme when he endorsed a gardening product on ITV during the mid-70s.

★ Actor Mark Moraghan, who plays Owen in *Holby City*, once posed naked in an advert for Complan.

★ The voice of Kelloggs Frosties' Tony the Tiger is provided by actor Thurl Ravenscroft.

★ Nick Berry made an early television appearance with his mum – they starred in an advert for Stork margarine.

★ Actress Claire Goose, who appeared in *Casualty* and *Waking the Dead*, also started off in adverts. She was the girl in the Wash 'n' Go shampoo advert who rinsed her hair in a fountain.

★ Sebastian Coe was the first British athlete to be allowed to use his own name to promote products on television when he advertised Horlicks in 1982.

★ In the mid-60s, broadcasters Jimmy Young and Valerie Singleton both sang the praises of the household cleaning product Flash.

★ *X-Files* star David Duchovny made his first professional appearance in a Lowenbrau beer commercial.

★ One of Kate Winslet's first screen roles was starring in an advert for Sugar Puffs.

★ One person who failed to make it in commercials was Jennifer Lopez, who was once turned down for a jeans advert because her bottom was considered to be too big.

FAMOUS LEFT HANDERS

In times gone by, left-handed people were thought to be the children of the devil. Children who showed signs of being left-handed had their arm tied behind their back while others had their hand chopped off! Luckily today's celebrity wacky-handers have not suffered the same fate.

Damon Albarn
Drew Barrymore
Kim Basinger
David Bowie
Pierce Brosnan
Julian Clary
Paul Daniels
Charlie Dimmock
Celine Dion
Bob Geldof
Susan Hampshire
Angelina Jolie
Ross Kemp
Kermit the Frog
Lisa Kudrow
Marshall Mathers
a.k.a. Eminem

Melinda Messenger
George Michael
Robert de Niro
Sarah Jessica Parker
Michael Parkinson
Fiona Phillips
Robert Redford
Keanu Reeves
Shane Richie
Jennifer Saunders
Julia Sawalha
Sting
Prince William
Oprah Winfrey

CELEBRITY LOVE

Celebs today only have to glance in the direction of a member of the opposite sex (or even the same sex), before newspapers start speculating on future marriage plans and the long-term compatibility of the couple.

Just a day after news broke that Geri Halliwell was seeing radio and TV presenter Chris Evans, some tabloids carried a picture of what the potential offspring of the artist formerly known as Ginger Spice and the 'Ginger Whinger' would look like. The ink was barely dry on the page when the couple split up!

Here are some facts about some of the successful and not so successful relationships of the famous.

★ As a young actress in the chorus line of *South Pacific*, *Absolutely Fabulous* star June Whitfield dated a young American actor called Larry Hagman, who went on to find fame in *Dallas*.

★ Television presenter Vanessa Feltz shared her first kiss with dance DJ Pete Tong.

★ Actress Jenny Agutter didn't live with a man until she married her husband Johan when she was 38.

★ Barbara Windsor had a romantic liaison with notorious gangster Reggie Kray in the 1960s and has also been associated with footballer George Best and Bee Gee Maurice Gibb – however, she turned down a date with Hollywood legend Warren Beatty.

★ Jeffrey Archer (father) and Dame Cleo Laine (mother) both had bigamous parents.

★ While they were still together, actors Billy Bob Thornton and Angelina Jolie demonstrated their love for each other by wearing amulets of each other's blood. They also presented each other with burial plots on their first wedding anniversary. When they separated Jolie demanded that her blood be returned.

★ Bond actor George Lazenby is married to former tennis player Pam Shriver.

★ Meg Matthews and Noel Gallagher, Richard Gere and Cindy Crawford, Bob Geldof and Paula Yates, and Chris Evans and Billie Piper all got married in The Little Church of the West in Las Vegas.

★ For four years during the 1980s, *Men Behaving Badly* star Leslie Ash went out with *Mr Bean* star Rowan Atkinson.

★ Terry Wogan and Ronan Keating were both virgins on their wedding day.

★ Elton John announced that 'I simply want to be a family man', when he married Renate Blauel in 1984. The marriage ended just four years later and soon afterwards Elton revealed that he was gay.

★ Actor Sean Penn was said to have been so annoyed by the press helicopters that hovered in the sky during his nuptials to Madonna, that he began firing a gun into the air.

★ BBC newsreader Anna Ford was once engaged to newsreader Jon Snow.

★ Television host Jonathan Ross and former 'It Girl' Tara Palmer-Tomkinson both lost their virginity at 21, while actor Dudley Moore reportedly had to wait until he was 23.

★ Elizabeth Taylor, Joan Collins, Barbara Windsor and Vivienne

Westwood have all married men who were more than twenty years younger than them.

★ Television presenter Nadia Sawalha met her husband Mark when she was presenting and he was directing a dating show called *Perfect Partners*. In 28 episodes they were the only couple that got together.

★ While performing at Warwick University before he rose to fame, Rod Stewart tried to chat up future cabinet minister Mo Mowlam. She rejected his advances.

★ Celine Dion first met her husband Rene Angelil when she was 12 and he was 38. She is three months younger than her stepson, Patrick Angelil.

★ When David Beckham first met his future wife Victoria, he was so worried about losing her phone number that he wrote it on 'six or seven' pieces of paper, which he put around the house.

★ Rolf Harris, Paul Newman, Sir John Mills and Tom Jones have all been married for more than forty years.

★ Veteran actress Carol Channing – best known for her role in the Broadway musical *Hello Dolly!* – married her childhood sweetheart Harry Kullijian when he was 83 and she was 82. When he heard that Channing had wanted to get in touch again after more than sixty years, Kullijian declared that he thought she was dead.

★ When Elizabeth Taylor married Larry Fortensky in 1991, she declared, 'This is it, forever.' Her marriage to the construction worker, who she met at the Betty Ford Clinic, ended in 1995.

★ When Madonna married Guy Ritchie, the minister who performed the ceremony presented the couple with a toilet roll, saying, 'It's long and strong, which is what I hope your marriage will be.'

★ Television presenter Davina McCall met her husband Matthew Robinson while walking her dog in her local park.

★ *GMTV* presenter Fiona Phillips celebrated her 1997 Las Vegas marriage to former reporter Martin Frizell with a gambling session. The pair spent their first evening as a married couple playing roulette, blackjack and the slot machines.

★ Both Demi Moore and Julia Roberts cancelled their weddings after the invitations had been sent out (Moore to Emilio Estevez, and Roberts to Kiefer Sutherland).

★ Actress Amanda Donohoe's first serious relationship was with Adam Ant.

★ Actress Drew Barrymore split from her first husband, Welsh-born bar owner Jeremy Thomas, after just nineteen days of marriage in 1994.

★ Cher filed for divorce from musician Greg Allman only nine days after marrying him.

★ Even shorter, actress Zsa Zsa Gabor's marriage to Felipe de Alba ended after eight days. He was her ninth husband.

★ Other celebrity couples who didn't reach their first anniversary include: Lisa Marie Presley and Nicolas Cage (three months), Jennifer Lopez and Cris Judd (eight months), Richard Burton and Liz Taylor (ten months), and actress Helen Hunt and *Simpson*'s actor Hank Azaria (eleven months).

★ Clark Gable was married five times.

★ In 1995 opera singer Pavarotti described his marriage as 'incredibly monogamous'. Only six months later it came to light that he was having an affair with his 26-year-old assistant.

ROMANCE ON THE SET

Romance at the workplace is common. Studies have found that over half of all men have slept with a work colleague, while almost 30 per cent of people have married or are in a relationship with someone they met while at work.

And just because celebrities don't have an office where they can make eyes at one another over the photocopier, it doesn't stop them getting jiggy with their colleagues and co-stars while on set – even if the relationships do not always last.

Richard Burton and Elizabeth Taylor – *Cleopatra*

Jude Law and Sadie Frost – *Shopping*

Paul Bettany and Jennifer Connolly – *A Beautiful Mind*

Tom Cruise and Nicole Kidman – *Days of Thunder*

Hugh Grant and Liz Hurley – *Rowing with the Wind*

Kurt Russell and Goldie Hawn – *Swing Shift*

Ralph Fiennes and Francesca Annis – *Hamlet*

Russell Crowe and Meg Ryan – *Proof of Life*

Greg Wise and Emma Thompson – *Sense and Sensibility*

Jim Carrey and Renee Zellweger – *Me, Myself and Irene*

Warren Beatty and Annette Benning – *Bugsy*

Tom Hanks and Rita Wilson – *The Volunteers*

Titanic director James Cameron and Linda Hamilton – *Terminator 2: Judgement Day*

Director Steven Spielberg and Kate Capshaw – *Indiana Jones and the Temple of Doom*

Assistant Director Jim Threapleton and Kate Winslet – *Hideous Kinky*

Alec Baldwin and Kim Basinger – *The Marrying Man*

Paul Hogan and Linda Kozlowski – *Crocodile Dundee*

Jonny Lee Miller and Angelina Jolie – *Hackers*

Dennis Quaid and Meg Ryan – *Innerspace*

Jeff Goldblum and Geena Davis – *The Fly*

Humphrey Bogart and Lauren Bacall – *To Have and Have Not*

Tim Robbins and Susan Sarandon - *Bull Durham*

Liam Neeson and Natasha Richardson – *Anna Christie* (Broadway production)

Charlie Sheen and Denise Richards – *Spin City*

Gary Hobbs (Ricky Groves) and Hannah Waterman (Laura Beale) – *EastEnders*

Ben Freeman (Scott Windsor) and Amy Nuttall (Chloe Atkinson) – *Emmerdale*

Matthew MacFadyen and Keeley Hawes – *Spooks*

Steve McFadden (Phil Mitchell) and Lucy Benjamin (Lisa Fowler) – *EastEnders*

Colin Firth and Jennifer Ehle – *Pride and Prejudice*

Peter Amory (Chris Tate) and Claire King (Kim Tate) – *Emmerdale*

★ CELEBRITY BODIES ★

With so many famous people baring all in front of the cameras for films and magazines, you might think that there isn't a lot you don't know about the seemingly perfect bodies of the famous.

However, read on and you might just learn a thing or two.

★ Barbara Windsor has size 1 feet.

★ Actress Daryl Hannah has size 11 feet.

★ Billy Connolly has pierced nipples.

★ Sean Connery has two small tattoos on his right arm. One says 'Mum and Dad', the other 'Scotland Forever'. He got them when he enlisted in the navy at the age of sixteen.

★ Roger Moore was a fat child, ridiculed for his obesity.

★ Frank Sinatra weighed 13lb when he was born. He was initially thought to have been stillborn until his grandmother held him under the cold-water tap. He had lacerated earlobes and cheeks as well as a punctured eardrum after forceps were used during the delivery.

★ Actor Leslie Nielsen, star of the *Naked Gun* films, is legally deaf.

★ *Star Trek's* Captain Jean-Luc Picard, actor Patrick Stewart, lost all his hair at the age of nineteen.

★ Actress Sadie Frost suffered a collapsed lung when she was four years old.

★ Michael Caine suffered from an eye disease that made his eyelids swell.

★ Actor and Sheffield United fan Sean Bean has a tattoo on his left bicep with the words '100% Blade', the Blades being the nickname of his beloved soccer team.

★ Publicist Max Clifford has suffered from epileptic fits.

★ Anthony Worrall Thompson's face was disfigured in a rugby scrum while at school. He had to wait until he was 21 to have plastic surgery, and spent twelve weeks in hospital afterwards.

★ Irish singer Samantha Mumba says she does 1,500 sit-ups a day to keep in shape.

★ Television presenter Ulrika Jonsson has a tattoo of a devil on her bottom.

★ Actor Peter Falk, who plays the raincoat-wearing detective Columbo, got his squinty gaze after losing an eye at the age of three.

★ Presenter Judy Finnegan contracted measles when she was five. It left her with a heart murmur that she still has today.

★ Rod Stewart is colour blind, as is snooker player Peter Ebdon.

★ Singer Anastacia and actor Jeff Hordley, who plays Cain Dingle in *Emmerdale*, both suffer from the potentially fatal bowel disorder Crohn's disease.

★ A salesperson at Fredericks of Hollywood confided in 1985 that Dolly Parton buys a size 36DD black push-up bra.

★ Comedian Joan Rivers has had so much plastic surgery that her grandson calls her 'Nana new Face'.

★ Actress Francesca Annis had her nose resculpted when she was 21, because she considered it to be 'too heavy looking'.

★ Actor Burt Reynolds was *Cosmopolitan*'s first male nude centrefold.

★ Jamie Oliver's career as a chef was almost cut short before it had begun. As a teenager, he severed an artery in his hand after picking up a tea towel that had been used to collect some broken china. One sharp piece went into his hand, and Oliver needed microsurgery to repair both the artery and a damaged nerve.

★ Singer and presenter Des O'Connor suffered from rickets as a child and spent most of his childhood with his legs in callipers. Doctors told him it was unlikely that he would ever walk.

★ Footballer-turned-presenter Ian Wright, *They Think it's All Over* presenter Nick Hancock and *EastEnders* actor Adam Woodyatt have all suffered from asthma.

★ *Bargain Hunt*'s David Dickinson has had the same hairstyle since 1969. He gets his exotic appearance from his mother who was half-Armenian and half-French.

★ Actress Nicole Kidman wore a corset during the filming of the 1996 film *Portrait of a Lady*, in order to reduce her waist to nineteen inches.

★ Nineteen inches would leave room to spare for fellow actress Winona Ryder. She can squeeze herself into seventeen-inch corsets if necessary.

★ Comedian and television presenter Brian Conley has a tattoo on his bottom, which says 'No Entry'.

★ Singer Ray Charles went blind at the age of eight after contracting glaucoma. He taught himself to compose by Braille while at a school for the blind.

★ Ken Dodd's famous protruding teeth were caused by a cycling accident when he was a child.

★ Robin Williams accidentally broke Robert de Niro's nose during the filming of *Awakenings*.

★ Winona Ryder's hair is naturally blonde. She dyed it black for her role in the 1986 film *Lucas*, and never went back to her roots.

★ Tom Jones, Edwina Currie, Dale Winton and *The Royle Family's* Caroline Aherne have all had nose jobs.

★ Film legend Humphrey Bogart's lisp was the result of an accident that happened while he was serving in the US Navy. His publicists always maintained that the injury was sustained when the ship upon which he was stationed was torpedoed. However, in reality it appears that a handcuffed prisoner who was trying to escape smacked Bogart in the mouth.

★ Entertainer and game-show host Bruce Forsyth only has one kidney. The other one was removed when he was 21.

★ As a child actor, Leonardo DiCaprio was rejected by a casting agent for having an 'inappropriate' haircut.

★ Larry Hagman, *Birds of a Feather* star Linda Robson and diet guru Rosemary Conley have all suffered from gallstones.

★ She may have been a voluptuous sex goddess as an adult, but as a skinny child Sophia Loren was nicknamed 'The Stick'.

★ Matt Damon lost three and a half stone for his role in *Courage under Fire*. He achieved this through extreme fasting and running thirteen miles a day.

★ Meanwhile, Robert de Niro put on over four stone for the role of Jake La Motta in Martin Scorsese's 1980 film *Raging Bull*.

★ When he was four, artist and *Animal Hospital* presenter Rolf Harris contracted scarlet fever, which saw him quarantined from his family for nearly six months. When he was declared well enough to see them, his ankles and legs were bowed, as he had been allowed to run around in hospital too early, after spending over a month in bed.

MISDEMEANOURS OF THE FAMOUS

Some people believe that celebrities and those in the public eye should set an example to the rest of us, and at all times behave like good, upstanding citizens.

Try telling that to these famous reprobates...

★ *Crimewatch* presenter Nick Ross was once on the front page of a national newspaper for committing a crime – he shoplifted sweets when he was eleven years old.

★ Singer and presenter Claire Sweeney stole a chocolate bar from a shop when she was eight. She ran home with it, only to find that the house had been broken into. She went upstairs and saw a pair of feet under the bed – the burglar was still in the house. She was convinced that this was the punishment for her crime.

★ Actor Johnny Depp was arrested in 1994 after trashing a $1200-a-night hotel room in New York.

★ Television presenter Johnny Vaughan spent four years in prison for drugs offences.

★ Actress and presenter Denise van Outen took an ashtray and a tissue-box holder from Buckingham Palace during a royal reception for a select group of young Britons. When the story hit the press, van Outen apologised and returned the items to the Queen.

★ *Men Behaving Badly* star Martin Clunes was once arrested for riding a moped on a golf course.

★ The Football Association suspended singer Craig David in 2000 for failing to pay an £18 fine he had picked up with his Sunday League team. His 'African And Caribbean' team left a Sunday parks league in January 1998 with a debt of £309 in unpaid fees for the hire of pitches.

★ *They Think it's All Over* presenter Nick Hancock was fined £40 by magistrates in Stafford after being caught fishing without a licence. When approached by BBC Radio 5Live to present a fishing programme, he thought he should confess to his crime. They told him they were already aware of his fine – that was how they knew that he fished!

★ *Scarface* actor Al Pacino was arrested for carrying a 'concealed weapon', a pistol, in 1961.

★ In 1992, former heavyweight boxing champion Mike Tyson was sentenced to six years in prison for the rape of beauty queen Desiree Washington.

★ Director Guy Ritchie received a police caution after kicking a fan who was hanging around outside his and Madonna's home in Notting Hill.

★ In 1998, cricketer Phil Tufnell was fined £800 for assaulting his girlfriend when she allegedly refused to let him see their daughter. He has also been fined £500 by the cricket authorities for kicking his cap and swearing while on tour in India.

★ Boxing promoter Don King served almost four years in prison in the 1960s after being found guilty of manslaughter.

★ When he was eight years old, MP John Prescott and friends set a field on fire after playing with matches. To teach him a lesson, his dad shopped him to the police.

★ Footballer-turned-actor Vinnie Jones was once fined £20,000 by the Football Association for taking part in a video in which he gave tips on how to foul players behind the referee's back.

★ *Thelma and Louise* star Susan Sarandon was arrested while still at high school for protesting against the Vietnam War.

★ In 1997, football-star-turned-actor OJ Simpson was found guilty in a civil trial of killing his former wife Nicole and her friend Ronald Goldman. Simpson was forced to pay the relatives of the deceased £20 million.

★ *Royle Family* star Ricky Tomlinson was jailed for two years for his part in the 1972 builders' strike, during which he organised flying pickets and refused to testify against his fellow strikers. He served his time in fourteen prisons, mostly in solitary confinement.

★ Kevin Spacey set his sister's tree house on fire when he was a child. He was sent to military academy, only to be thrown out later.

★ Jockey Lester Piggott was jailed for three years in 1987 after admitting tax evasion totalling £3.1 million. He served one year. As a result of his criminal conviction, he was forced to hand back his OBE.

★ Football manager Brian Clough was fined £5,000 in 1989 after being accused of hitting four fans.

★ Actress Sophia Loren also served time for tax evasion in 1982, but it was only seventeen days.

★ In 1998, Mötley Crüe drummer Tommy Lee was jailed for six months after beating up his wife Pamela Anderson.

★ Bee Gee Barry Gibb was put on probation for two months when he was a child, after being blamed for stealing a car. His mother was so concerned that he and his brothers would end up in serious trouble that she decided the family should emigrate to Australia.

★ In 1999 police cautioned singing legend Diana Ross after an assault on a security officer at Heathrow Airport. The assault took place when the officer attempted to body-search Ross just before she boarded her plane. Ross later said it was a 'natural instinct' to fight back when humiliated.

★ Singer Courtney Love got into trouble at Heathrow Airport. Love was arrested in February 2003 after accusations of verbally abusing crewmembers during a flight from Los Angeles to London. She had tried to move her nurse into first class while in the air, and a stewardess had objected. She was later released with a caution for 'causing harassment, alarm and distress', after spending nine hours in custody.

★ French actor Gerard Depardieu was regarded as something of a juvenile delinquent during his early years, spending much of his childhood involved in petty theft. It took a social worker to sort him out and persuade him to direct his energies into acting. Depardieu has said that if he hadn't become an actor, he probably would have become a killer.

★ Actor Neil Morrissey was charged with pilfering when he was ten years old. He was sent away to children's homes for seven years.

★ In 1999, former cabinet minister Jonathan Aitken was sentenced to eighteen months in prison after pleading guilty to charges of perjury and perverting the course of justice, following the collapse of his libel case against the *Guardian* and the makers of the ITV programme *World in Action*.

★ Victoria Beckham had to pay £55,000 in damages to an autograph and memorabilia shop owner, over a disputed autograph of her husband. On visiting the shop, Victoria had seen a picture of husband David in a display cabinet at the entrance, which was autographed by the footballer. Victoria thought it was not genuine, and said so in the shop. After reports of her visits appeared in the press, the owners decided to sue for slander.

★ In 1988, *Frasier* star Kelsey Grammer was sent to prison for two weeks after failing to complete the community service that he had been given for drug offences.

★ Legendary footballer George Best served twelve weeks in prison in 1984 after being caught drink-driving.

★ In 2002 a court fined Princess Anne £500 and ordered her to pay £500 compensation after one of her dogs attacked two children. It was the first time a senior member of the Royal Family had been convicted of a criminal offence, and the first time a senior member of the Royal Family had attended court for over one hundred years.

★ Hugh Grant was fined £700 for his 'lewd conduct' with Los Angeles prostitute Divine Brown in 1995.

★ Hollywood actor Charlie Sheen was arrested for credit-card fraud and possessing marijuana while he was still at school. He was also found guilty of buying exam answers.

★ *EastEnder's* Dirty Den, actor Leslie Grantham, served eleven years in prison for shooting dead a taxi driver while he was serving as a soldier in Germany in the 1960s. Grantham had been attempting to rob the driver and, while threatening him with a gun, had ended up killing him.

★ Singer Dame Shirley Bassey was arrested in 1978 for being drunk and disorderly, after pushing a policeman who had complained about the noise coming from one of her parties.

★ Former *Coronation Street* actress Tracy Shaw was once caught shoplifting. She put the offence down to simple absent-mindedness, and no charges were pressed.

★ Noel Gallagher from Oasis was put on six months' probation when he was a teenager, after being caught stealing from a corner shop.

★ Paul McCartney spent nine days in a Japanese prison for possessing drugs in 1980.

★ *Cold Feet* star James Nesbitt admitted once spending the night in prison after being caught urinating in a public place.

★ Fellow *Cold Feet* star John Thomson was banned from driving for three years after admitting drink-driving. He told officers who breathalysed him, 'it's a fair cop', when they stopped his car.

★ Jim Morrison, lead singer of the 60s rock group The Doors, was the first rock star to be arrested on stage.

★ Actor Sean Penn spent 32 days in prison in 1987 for hitting a man who had kissed his then wife, Madonna. He later violated his probation by hitting out at two photographers he caught snooping around his apartment.

★ The only illegal aspect of singer Jerry Lee Lewis's marriage to his thirteen-year-old second cousin, was that he hadn't divorced his previous wife.

★ Keanu Reeves was arrested for drink-driving in 1993.

★ Oscar winner Halle Berry was placed on three years' probation, fined $13,500 and ordered to do 200 hours community service after being found guilty in 2000 of jumping a red traffic light, hitting another car and leaving the scene of the accident.

★ Jodie Foster was put on one year's probation in 1983 after being caught in possession of cocaine.

★ David Dickinson was sent to Strangeways prison in Manchester when he was nineteen, after being found guilty of mail-order fraud.

★ TV chef James Martin has admitted he used to deliberately damage supermarket stock to get the price reduced. He reportedly used to stamp on food to save money as a student.

★ Writer and comedian Stephen Fry was jailed for credit-card fraud when he was eighteen. He was caught after arousing the suspicions of a hotel receptionist in Swindon. She had questioned why a boy who wore shabby shoes was in possession of several plastic cards. Fry was put on probation for two years and spent two months inside while police attended to his case.

★ *Auf Wiedersehen, Pet* star Jimmy Nail spent four months in Strangeways prison after a fight at a football match.

★ Before becoming known as the 'Walrus of Love', soul singer Barry White was imprisoned for car theft.

★ Actor and comedian Bob Hope was briefly jailed when he was young for stealing tennis balls and racquets from a sports shop.

★ In 2001 novelist and former MP Jeffrey Archer was jailed for four years after being found guilty of perjury and perverting the course of justice. Charges arose from his successful 1987 libel action, in which he won £500,000 damages from the *Daily Star* over allegations that he slept with a prostitute. He was found guilty of asking his former friend Ted Francis to provide him with a false alibi for a night relating to the libel case, and of producing fake diary entries to back up his story.

★ DJ Goldie has admitted he used to shoplift from Burton menswear – the fashion chain he later became the face of. He said that by agreeing to help out with an advertising campaign, he was giving something back to the store he once took from.

★ *Inspector Morse* star Kevin Whately found himself on the wrong side of the law in his younger days. He was arrested twice for busking on the underground.

★ *Ally McBeal* and film star Robert Downey Jnr was jailed for three years in 1999 for breaking probation relating to previous drugs offences. He served one year. During his time in prison, however, he was still allowed to appear in the film *Friends and Lovers*. Studio bosses were given permission to fly him from his prison to Utah for filming, as long as Downey Jnr was returned to the jail by 11 p.m. each night.

★ Ben Affleck was fined $135 in 1999 for driving in Massachusetts with a suspended licence.

★ *Trigger Happy TV* star Dom Joly has been arrested in Switzerland while pretending to be a yeti, in Belgium for impersonating an English policeman, and in the Empire State Building while filming a sequence in which he was a spy.

★ Whitney Houston and husband Bobby Brown were once banned from a hotel in California after causing £18,700 worth of damage to their room.

★ In 1962 actress Sophia Loren and Carlo Ponti were charged with bigamy.

★ Singer Ozzy Osbourne was put in prison and banned from Texas for ten years after urinating on the revered Alamo fort in San Antonio. He was wearing a dress at the time. He has also spent six weeks in Birmingham's Winson Green prison in 1966, after being caught stealing a television. The police were also called after a stoned Ozzy once attempted to murder his wife and manager, Sharon, while on tour in Moscow. No charges were brought.

★ Isaac Hayes, best known for his 'Theme from *Shaft*' was sent to prison in 1989 for failing to pay $346,000 in child support and alimony.

★ In 1992 Gordon Banks, England's goalkeeper in their 1966 World Cup triumph, was accused of selling FA Cup tickets on the black market. He was banned from receiving any more for ten years.

★ Fellow footballer and Manchester United star Eric Cantona was sentenced to 120 hours of community service, as well as being fined by the FA and banned from playing for eight months, after kung-fu kicking a Crystal Palace fan who was verbally abusing him from the crowd, during a game between the two teams.

★ Actress Winona Ryder was put on probation for three years, fined £6,000 and ordered to do 480 hours of community service after being found guilty of stealing almost £4,000-worth of clothes from an upmarket Beverly Hills store.

★ Nightclub owner Peter Stringfellow spent a short time in prison when he was twenty, after being found guilty of selling stolen goods.

★ Actor Steve McQueen spent 41 days in a US forces prison after going AWOL while serving in the marines in 1947.

★ In 2002, 80s pop star Adam Ant was placed under a twelve-month community rehabilitation order and ordered to pay £500 compensation to an injured pub musician after admitting one charge of affray. He had smashed a pub window – injuring the musician – and waved a pistol at customers who ran after him, after drinkers had laughed as his 'cowboy' clothes.

★ The Rolling Stones were fined £5 in 1965 for urinating against the wall of a petrol station.

★ In 1989 *West Wing* star Rob Lowe was arrested and accused of videoing his sexual activities with an under-aged girl. He was punished with community service.

ANAGRAMS OF FAMOUS NAMES

Sometimes rearranging the letters of a celebrity's name reveals more about them than they would wish.

Tony Blair PM – I'm Tory Plan B

Kylie Minogue – I Like 'Em Young

Mariah Carey – Hairy Camera

Ronan Keating – A Grannie Knot

Britney Spears – Nip Yer Breasts

Christine Hamilton – Hitler in Macintosh

Vanessa Paradis – A Spaniards Vase

George Michael – I Come, He Gargle

Darren Day – Randy Dear

Margaret Thatcher – That Great Charmer

Christopher Evans – He's a rich TV person

Nicole Kidman – Nicknamed Oil

Arnold Schwarzenegger – I've Grown Large 'n' Crazed

Tara Palmer-Tomkinson – 'I'm a Plonker' Moans Tart

Rod Stewart – Two Retards

Richard Madeley – Dreary Mild Ache

Mel Gibson – Big Melons

Paul Merton – Manure Plot

Diego Maradona – O Dear, I'm A Gonad

Martine McCutcheon – NEC Concert a hit, Mum!

Michael Palin – A Pill Machine

Ewan McGregor – Gorge Crewman

Whitney Houston – Why Not Shine Out?

Gaby Roslin – Angry Boils

Robbie Williams – I Mobilise Brawl

Jennifer Lopez – Jeez! Elfin Porn

Sir David Attenborough – Horrid Bug Devastation

Chris Rea – Rich Arse

Gloria Hunniford – Fun Hairdo On Girl

Alan Titchmarsh – That Snail Charm

Calista Flockhart – LA Chick Farts A Lot

Michael Jackson – Also Chicken Jam

Martin Clunes – Internal Scum

Anne Robinson – No Brains, None

Gillian Anderson – Alien's DNA On Girl

Woody Allen – A Lewd Loony

Melinda Messenger – Smile Deranges Men

Monica Lewinsky – Saw Money In Lick

Hillary Clinton – Only I Can Thrill

Elizabeth Taylor – I, The Lazy Bloater

Elvis – Lives

Clint Eastwood – Old West Action

CELEBRITY ACHIEVEMENTS

Barely a week goes by without celebrities putting on their best frocks and walking down the red carpet for yet another back-slapping awards ceremony. But away from the Oscars, the Brits, the Golden Globes, the BAFTAs, the National Television Awards and the Grammys – which famous people really have an achievement to be proud of?

★ Radio presenter Paul Gambaccini was at Oxford University at the same time as former US President Bill Clinton. It was he, and not Clinton, who was voted 'The American Most Likely to Succeed'.

★ *Who Wants to be a Millionaire?* presenter Chris Tarrant was once the Beckenham Yard of Ale Drinking Champion.

★ *Thelma and Louise* star Susan Sarandon was once given the accolade of 'Celebrity Breasts of Summer', by *Playboy* magazine.

★ Warren Beatty is the only person in Oscar® history to have been nominated in the producer, director, writer and actor categories, all for the same film. Furthermore he has achieved this distinction twice – for *Heaven Can Wait* in 1978, and for *Reds* in 1981, for which he won the Best Director award.

★ Sarah Lancashire, Anita Dobson, Ulrika Jonsson, Charlotte Church, Melinda Messenger and Denise van Outen have all been named female Rear of the Year. Graham Norton, Robbie Williams, Frank Skinner and Gary Barlow have all picked up the award for the male equivalent.

★ Racing driver Stirling Moss won the British Lawnmower grand prix twice in the 1970s.

★ Jennifer Aniston, Bryan Ferry and Vic Reeves have all had their paintings exhibited.

★ In 1925 Charlie Chaplin was the first actor to appear on the cover of *Time* magazine.

★ Justin Timberlake once won a 'Dance Like New Kids on the Block' competition.

★ Sean Connery entered the 1953 Mr Universe competition. He came third in the tall man's division.

★ *The Fast Show*'s Paul Whitehouse was a former Baby Smile of the Rhondda Valley winner.

★ Carol Smillie was once the proud recipient of the title Miss Parallel Bars.

★ In 1947 Marilyn Monroe was chosen as the first Miss California Artichoke Queen.

★ Darius Danesh has an honorary degree in English Literature from Edinburgh University. Darius left his course in the third year to appear on *Pop Idol* and had always planned to go back to university to finish the degree, but his career took off and he never returned.

★ Before she was a member of the band S Club, Rachel Stevens won a *Just 17* magazine modelling competition.

★ Victoria Beckham picked up the cookery prize at school.

★ Tom Hanks was the first film star to be honoured with the US Navy Distinguished Public Service Award, for his film *Saving Private Ryan*.

★ Politician Mo Mowlam was awarded the Duke of Edinburgh's Gold Award.

★ Stephen Fry, Eric Morecambe, Tony Benn and Russ Abbott have all been honoured with the title Pipe Smoker of the Year.

★ Writer and broadcaster Gyles Brandreth was once European Monopoly champion.

★ Actress Elizabeth Taylor has appeared on the cover of *Life* magazine more than anyone else.

★ Jenny Eclair is the only woman to win the prestigious Perrier Award for comedy, which she did in 1995.

★ *The League of Gentlemen* cast won the 1997 Perrier Award for comedy, narrowly beating Graham Norton.

★ Michelle Pfeiffer once held the title of Miss Orange County.

★ Actress Pam St Clement, *EastEnders'* Pat Evans, is a member of the Institute of Advanced Motorists.

★ *Blackadder* and *Mr Bean* star Rowan Atkinson holds an HGV licence.

★ Ronan Keating, *GMTV* presenter Lorraine Kelly, Sir Cliff Richard, former Spice Girl Mel B and Prime Minister Tony Blair have all been named Spectacle Wearer of the Year.

★ Meanwhile, the Guild of British Tie Makers has, at various times, named Wendy Richard, Barry Norman, Des Lynam, Trevor McDonald and John Prescott Tie Wearer of the Year.

★ Actress Cybill Shepherd won the title of Miss Teenage Memphis when she was sixteen years old. Her prize was a wardrobe of clothes and one year's supply of Dr Pepper. She went on to represent Memphis in the Miss Teenage America pageant and, although she didn't win, she was presented with the title of Miss Congeniality.

★ Catherine Zeta Jones was once British Tap Dancing Champion.

THE REAL NAMES OF
THE FAMOUS

They say you can choose your friends, but you can't choose your family. Another thing you can't choose is the name you are born with. However, that doesn't mean that you have to like it or keep it. Some celebrities believe that changing their name really will help bring them success.

Judging by some of the names these stars were born with, you can see their point.

★ Singer Tom Jones was born Thomas Woodward Junior. His mother's maiden name was Jones, even though he actually took his name from the 1963 film *Tom Jones* starring Albert Finney.

★ David Jason was born David White. His twin brother, named Jason, died at birth.

★ Julia Roberts changed her name from Julie, as there was already an actress named Julie Roberts.

★ *Beetlejuice* star Michael Keaton was also forced to change his name as an existing actor shared his real name – Michael Douglas.

★ The same thing happened to David Bowie. His real name is David Jones, similar to the Monkees star Davy Jones.

★ *Coronation Street* and *Bad Girls* star, actress Amanda Barrie, was born Shirley Broadbent. She chose the name Barrie in honour of JM Barrie, because she loved Peter Pan.

★ Musician Moby's real name is Richard Melville Hall. He was nicknamed Moby because of the fact that he can trace his ancestry back to the author of *Moby Dick*, Herman Melville.

★ Martial arts film star Jackie Chan's name at birth was Chan Kong-sang. It means 'born in Hong Kong'.

★ Michael Caine was born Maurice Micklewhite. He changed his name after watching *The Caine Mutiny*.

★ Golfer Tiger Woods was actually given the Christian name Eldrick at birth. He was nicknamed 'Tiger' by his father, who was a lieutenant colonel in the US Army, after a Vietnamese soldier and friend who saved his father's life.

★ Rapper Eminem was born Marshall Mathers. He took his performance name from his initials MM – M&M.

★ Sigourney Weaver used to be known as Susan Alexandra Weaver. She chose her name from the novel *The Great Gatsby* in the hope that it would bring strange and exciting things into her life.

★ U2 front man Bono was born Paul Hewson. He took his name from a Dublin hearing aid shop called 'Bono Vox', which means 'Good Voice' in Latin.

★ Hell-raising Hollywood star Mickey Rourke's Christian name is actually Philip. He was nicknamed Mickey after the mouse.

★ *Harry Potter* author Joanne Rowling does not have a middle name. The initial 'K' came from her maternal grandmother Kathleen. It was her literary agent Christopher Little who suggested that Joanne became JK Rowling. He had heard from children's publishers that, while girls would read books written by men, boys would not read books written by women, so it would be best if she was known by an initial and a surname. 'J Rowling' was not considered to sound substantial enough, so the 'K' was added.

★ Singer Elvis Costello was born Declan McManus. He took on

his stage name when he signed to his first record company in 1977. He called himself Elvis after Elvis Presley, while Costello was his mother's maiden name.

★ *Some Mothers Do 'Ave 'Em* star Michael Crawford was born Michael Patrick Dumbell-Smith. He changed his name at the age of thirteen after seeing an advert proclaiming 'Crawford's Biscuits are Best'.

★ Actress Sissy Spacek was originally known as Mary Elizabeth Spacek. She was nicknamed 'Sissy' by her older brother and it stuck.

★ When he played in a jazz band, Gordon Sumner used to wear a yellow-and-black striped shirt and he looked like a bee. He was nicknamed 'Sting', and the name stuck.

★ Singer Diana Ross was originally known as 'Diane'. Motown record boss Berry Gordy made her change her name as he thought 'Diana' sounded classier.

★ Nicolas Cage was born Nicolas Coppola, the nephew of Francis Ford Coppola. After having worked on several films, he decided he didn't want to use his family name because of the expectations attached to it. He chose 'Cage' in honour of comic-book superhero Luke Cage and the composer John Cage.

★ Robbie Coltrane was born Robert MacMillan. He changed his name to Coltrane after the saxophonist John Coltrane.

★ Fashion guru Trinny Woodall was born with the Christian names Sarah Jane. She got her nickname after cutting off a classmate's pigtail. The creator of *St Trinian's*, Ronald Searle, was a friend of Trinny's father and told her, 'You're just like a St Trinian's girl.'

★ Singer Johnny Cash was born JR Cash. He chose the first name John when the military wouldn't accept just initials on its forms.

★ DJ Goldie's real name is Clifford Price. He earned his nickname not for his gold teeth, but from his gold dreadlocks that he cut off in the 1980s.

★ Reginald Kenneth Dwight chose the name Elton John after playing in a blues band with saxophonist Elton Dean and Long John Baldry.

★ *Emmerdale* and *Bad Girls* star Claire King was born Jayne Seed, but changed her surname to King because she was a massive fan of Elvis Presley.

★ Comedian Jenny Eclair was born Jenny Hargreaves. She is said to have changed it to Eclair after pretending to be French at a Blackpool nightclub.

★ Clive James was originally known as Vivien James, named after the 1938 Davis Cup player Vivien McGrath. After the success of *Gone with the Wind* with Vivien Leigh, Vivien became regarded as a girl's name, so he and his mother decided he should become known as Clive, after a Tyrone Power film featuring a character with that name.

★ *EastEnders*' Ricky Butcher, actor Sid Owen, was named David Sutton originally. He was reportedly nicknamed Sidney because he was plump as a child, and it rhymed with kidney, as in steak and kidney pie.

★ Comedian Frank Skinner was born Chris Collins. He took his stage name from a member of his local dominoes team.

★ Singer Shania Twain was still known as Eileen Twain when Mercury records in Nashville signed her. She decided to change it to Shania, which means 'I'm on my way' in Djibway, the tribe to which her father belonged.

★ John Cleese's family surname was Cheese. His father

changed it to Cleese to avoid being ridiculed when he enlisted in World War I.

★ Acting legend Richard Burton was christened Richard Jenkins. Burton was the surname of his drama teacher, who persuaded his father not to send him down the mines, but to allow Richard to move in with him and learn to be an actor.

★ Actor Shane Richie's real name is Shane Patrick Roche. It was Lenny Henry who persuaded him to change his name to Richie, when they toured together when Shane was seventeen. Until that point he had been using the stage name Shane Skywalker.

★ Liam Neeson was born William John Neeson. He became Liam because his sisters were unable to pronounce the word William when they were young.

★ Actress Whoopi Goldberg was born Caryn Johnson. She was called 'Whoopi cushion' as a child because of a severe flatulence problem!

Other stars who have changed their names include:

Isidore Danielovich Demsky – Kirk Douglas

Jennifer Anistopoulou – Jennifer Aniston

Mandy Rogers – Portia de Rossi

Anthony Benedetto – Tony Bennett

Enrique Martin Morales IV – Ricky Martin

John Frances Bongiovi Jnr – Jon Bon Jovi

Andrew Clutterbuck – Andrew Lincoln (*This Life, Teachers*)

John Robert Parker Ravenscroft – John Peel

Thomas Cruise Mapother IV – Tom Cruise

Amelia Driver – Minnie Driver

Barry Alan Pincus – Barry Manilow

Julie Harris – Patsy Palmer

Sylvia Butterfield – Liz Dawn (Vera Duckworth in *Coronation Street*)

Niomi McLean-Daley – Ms Dynamite

Cornell Haynes Jnr – Rapper Nelly

Nigel Neill – Sam Neill

Priscilla Marie Veronica White – Cilla Black

Julie Elizabeth Wells – Julie Andrews

Ilyena Mironoff – Helen Mirren

Eleanor Nancy Gow – Elle Macpherson

James Michael Aloysius Bradford – Jimmy Nail

Jim Moir – Vic Reeves

Vincent Damon Furnier –Alice Cooper

Anna Maria Louise Italiano – Anne Bancroft

Roger Davis – Jasper Carrott

Daniel Agraluscarsacra – Dan Aykroyd

Joyce Penelope Wilhelmina Frankenberg – Jane Seymour

Camille Javal – Brigitte Bardot

David Evans – The Edge (U2)

Thomas Connery – Sean Connery

Audrey Faith Perry – Faith Hill

Susan Stockard – Stockard Channing (*The West Wing*)

Henry Warren Beatty – Warren Beatty

Georgios Kyriacos Panayiotou – George Michael

Goldie Studlenghawn – Goldie Hawn

Winona Horowitz – Winona Ryder

Quentin Cook – Norman Cook (Fatboy Slim)

Cherilyn LaPiere Sarkisan – Cher

Marie McDonald McLaughlin Lawrie – Lulu

Helen Adu – Sade

Susan Tomaling – Susan Sarandon

Alicia Christian Foster – Jodie Foster

Leslie Hestletine – Les Dennis

Orville Burrell – Shaggy

Krishna Banji – Ben Kingsley

Ramon Estevez – Martin Sheen

Carlos Irwin Estevez – Charlie Sheen

Graham William Walker – Graham Norton

Michael Blake Day-Lewis – Daniel Day-Lewis

Alecia Moore – Pink

John Charles Carter – Charlton Heston

Annie Mae Bullock – Tina Turner

Cameron Davidson – Jim Davidson

Demetria Guynes – Demi Moore

Eric Patrick Clapp – Eric Clapton

Margaret Mary Emily Anne Hyra – Meg Ryan

Walter Willison – Bruce Willis

★ Neil Diamond is actually his real name, but at the beginning of his career the singer thought about calling himself Noah Kaminsky.

★ A talent agent once suggested to Leonardo DiCaprio that he change his name to Lenny Williams. DiCaprio declined.

★ In 2002, an American journalist claimed he had been contacted by lawyers representing former Rolling Stones member Bill Wyman over the use of his name, which happened to be the same as the guitarist. Journalist Bill Wyman, a staff writer for the *Atlanta Journal-Constitution*, said the guitarist threatened legal action over the use of his name, unless he could prove that he had come by it legally. He also demanded that the journalist added a disclaimer to everything he wrote in the future, 'clearly indicating that he was not the same Bill Wyman who was a member of the Rolling Stones'. The former Stone was actually born William George Perks, and changed his name to Bill Wyman by deed poll in 1964, three years *after* the journalist was born.

CELEBRITY REDCOATS

Not all of today's performers started their career on a reality TV show. Some learned their trade the hard way.

Johnny Ball	Des O'Connor
Michael Barrymore	Cliff Richard
Darren Day	Ted Rogers
'H' from Steps	William G Stewart
Bill Maynard	Jimmy Tarbuck

And, while they weren't redcoats, other celebrities got their break at Butlins.

★ Status Quo formed at Minehead Butlins.

★ *Chicago* actress Catherine Zeta Jones and Les Dennis both appeared in Butlin's talent shows. Zeta Jones took the top prize in her competition when she was ten years old.

★ Beatle Ringo Starr played in his first band – Rory Storm and the Hurricanes – at Pwllheli Butlins.

★ Actress-turned-MP Glenda Jackson once worked in a coffee bar at Butlins in Filey.

★ *EastEnders*' Shane Richie and *Coronation Street's* Janice Battersby, actress Vicky Entwistle, were both Pontin's Blue Coats.

★ ★ ★ ★ ★ ★ ★ ★ ★ ★ ★ ★ ★ ★ ★ ★ ★ ★ ★
CELEBRITY CONNECTIONS
★ ★ ★ ★ ★ ★ ★ ★ ★ ★ ★ ★ ★ ★ ★ ★ ★ ★ ★

All famous people appear to know one another. They are always being pictured kissing one another on the cheek, or deep in conversation at showbiz parties.

The truth is that most of the time they probably only know as much about their fellow celebrities as we do, and are just being friendly in order to find out the latest gossip and make sure they are not missing out on any good jobs.

Some celebrities, however, do have real showbiz connections.

★ Sophie, the Countess of Wessex, once dated Michael Parkinson's son.

★ Both Jack Nicholson and Eric Clapton grew up not knowing that their sister was actually their mother.

★ *Channel 4 News* presenter Jon Snow used to share a flat with American poet and author Maya Angelou.

★ Tom Hanks is a direct descendent of Nancy Hanks, the mother of Abraham Lincoln.

★ Singers Neil Diamond and Neil Sedaka went to the same high school.

★ Singer Liza Minnelli and actress Mia Farrow were childhood playmates.

★ Anthony Hopkins, *Lovejoy* star Ian McShane and *Elephant Man* star John Hurt, were all classmates at RADA.

★ Laurence Llewelyn-Bowen claims he is descended from Merlin, King Arthur's magician.

★ One of Terry Wogan's researchers on his first television chat show was Jeremy Beadle.

★ Actress Winona Ryder was the goddaughter of LSD guru Dr Timothy Leary.

★ When actress Prunella Scales married fellow actor Timothy West in Chelsea Register Office in 1963, the hat she wore belonged to the wife of Andrew Sachs. Scales and Sachs, of course, later went on to star together in *Fawlty Towers*.

★ Damon Hill's dad, racing driver Graham Hill, taught Prince Andrew to drive.

★ Tom Jones got his big break from Joe Collins, the father of Joan and Jackie Collins. Collins put Jones on the bill for his first concert tour in 1964.

★ Geri Halliwell, actresses Sandra Bullock and Cameron Diaz, as well as heart-throbs George Clooney and Russell Crowe, all enjoy knitting.

★ *Phoenix Nights* star Peter Kay was taught metalwork at school by Steve Coogan's dad.

★ David Beckham and *EastEnder's* Martin Fowler, actor James Alexandrou, both attended the same school in Chingford in Essex.

★ The mother of *Friends* star David Schwimmer was the attorney who handled Roseanne Barr's first divorce.

★ When Billy Crystal was studying cinema at New York University, *Gangs of New York* director Martin Scorsese was one of his professors.

★ The father of Nick Pickard, who plays Tony Hutchinson in *Hollyoaks*, is the ITV1 Head of Programmes Nigel Pickard.

★ Angela, the mother of actors James and Edward Fox, was the inspiration for the Noel Coward song 'Don't Put Your Daughter on the Stage, Mrs Worthington'.

★ During the filming of *Never Say Never Again*, Sean Connery took martial arts lessons, and had his wrist broken by his martial arts instructor after Connery allegedly angered him one day. The instructor was Steven Seagal.

★ The great-uncle of acting brothers Paul, Mark, Joe and Stephen McGann was James McGann, who was a survivor from the *Titantic*.

★ John Travolta, Kirstie Alley, Lisa Marie Presley and Tom Cruise are all followers of The Church of Scientology.

★ Steve McQueen and film director Roman Polanski were both given karate lessons by Bruce Lee.

★ When footballer Dwight Yorke was growing up in Trinidad, one of his best friends was legendary cricketer Brian Lara.

★ *Smack the Pony*'s Fiona Allen is the granddaughter of Britain's last hangman, Harry Allen. He was the public executioner at the hangings of James Hanratty, Derek Bentley and Ruth Ellis.

★ *TOTP* presenter Richard Blackwood's father was once married to Naomi Campbell's mother.

★ Singer Holly Valance is related to Benny Hill. Valance's maternal grandfather was Benny's first cousin.

★ Tara Palmer-Tomkinson's godfather is Prince Charles.

★ Eccentric history TV presenter Adam Hart-Davis is the great-great-great-grandson of William IV by his mistress Dora Jordan, which makes Queen Victoria his cousin five times removed.

★ Sammy Davis Jnr died on the same day as *Muppet Show*

creator Jim Henson.

★ Writer Virginia Wolfe mentions Harry Enfield's communist-supporting family in her diaries. She wrote that she would rather be dead in a field than have tea with the Enfields.

★ *Newsnight* presenter Jeremy Paxman, Judy Finnegan, *This Morning's* Fern Britton, actor Robert de Niro and *999* presenter Michael Buerk are all the parents of twins.

★ Director Steven Spielberg is Drew Barrymore's godfather. After seeing her pose naked in *Playboy* magazine, he sent her a blanket with a note telling her to cover herself up.

★ CBBC presenter Angellica Bell went to school with *Blue Peter* presenter Konnie Huq.

★ Uri Geller is related to Sigmund Freud.

★ Dolly Parton and Jerry Hall are both part Cherokee.

★ When Arnold Schwarzenegger won the Mr Universe title in 1967, one of the judges was Jimmy Saville.

★ Actor Tommy Lee Jones and former vice-president Al Gore were freshmen roommates at Harvard.

★ Michael Caine used to share a flat with the actor Terence Stamp when they were both beginning their acting careers.

★ Marlon Brando's son Miko was Michael Jackson's bodyguard.

★ Sir Cliff Richard, Francis Ford Coppola, *Grease* star Olivia Newton John, golfer Greg Norman and actor Sam Neill all have their own wine labels.

★ Nicholas Parsons' father was the GP who delivered Margaret Thatcher.

★ Legendary jazz singer Billie Holliday used to baby-sit for *When Harry Met Sally* star Billy Crystal when he was a child.

★ Former Prime Minister Margaret Thatcher, singer Christina Aguilera and Joan Collins are all afraid of the dark.

★ *What Not to Wear* presenter Susannah Constantine dated Princess Margaret's son Viscount Linley for over five years.

★ Actor Jeremy Irons's best man was Christopher Biggins.

FAMOUS PEOPLE WHO WERE ONCE GIRL GUIDES

All these celebrities used to gather around the campfire.

Mariah Carey

Judith Chalmers

Hillary Clinton

Gloria Hunniford

Glenda Jackson

Kathleen Turner

Kim Wilde

Venus Williams

★★★★★★★★★★★★★★★★★ FAMOUS RELATIONS

Some people would say that it would be bad enough having one showbiz luvvie in the family – but imagine if you had two! Just think ... double the tantrums, double the self-obsessing, double the time spent in front of the mirror, double the amount of scandal in the papers ... aarrgghhh!

★ Nicolas Cage's uncle is Francis Ford Coppola.

★ Comedian Jasper Carrott's daughter is *The Office's* Lucy Davis.

★ Sophie Ellis-Bextor's mother is former *Blue Peter* presenter Janet Ellis.

★ *Fat Friends'* actress Gaynor Faye's mother is *Fat Friends* and *Playing the Field* writer Kay Mellor.

★ Oscar-winning actress Hilary Swank is *West Wing* actor Rob Lowe's sister-in-law.

★ Keith Chegwin's sister is Radio 2 presenter Janice Long.

★ Actors Warren Beatty and Shirley MacLaine are brother and sister.

★ *Lord of the Rings* star Christopher Lee and James Bond creator Ian Fleming were cousins. Lee was Fleming's first choice to play the title role in the first Bond film, Dr No.

★ Actress Nanette Newman is the mother of radio and television presenter Emma Forbes.

★ Ralph and Joseph Fiennes are cousins of the explorer Sir Rannulph Fiennes.

★ Zoe Ball's father is children's programme *Think of a Number* presenter, Johnny Ball.

★ Actress Emma Thompson's father was Eric Thompson, who narrated *The Magic Roundabout*. Her mother is the actress Phyllida Law, and her sister Sophie appeared in *Four Weddings and a Funeral*.

★ *Shoestring* and *Waking the Dead* actor Trevor Eve is married to actress Sharon Maughan, who is best remembered as being one half of the 1980s 'Gold Blend Couple' and now appears in *Holby City*.

★ Singing wild boy Ashley Hamilton is the son of perma-tanned actor George Hamilton IV and Alana Stewart. Rod Stewart was his stepdad at one time.

★ Actress Helena Bonham Carter is the great-granddaughter of British Prime Minister Lord Herbert Asquith.

★ *Absolutely Fabulous* star Julia Sawalha and television presenter Nadia Sawalha are sisters.

★ Actress Joely Richardson is the daughter of fellow actress Vanessa Redgrave.

★ Laila Morse, who plays Mo in *EastEnders*, is actor Gary Oldman's sister.

★ Television presenters Jonathan Ross and Paul Ross are brothers. Their mum is a regular extra in *EastEnders* – she is one of the stallholders in the market.

★ Prime Minister Tony Blair and former PM Baroness Thatcher are distant cousins.

★ Former *RI:SE* presenter Mark Durden-Smith is the son of *Wish You Were Here* presenter Judith Chalmers.

★ Socialite and friend of Liz Hurley, Henry Dent Brocklehurst, is the godson of Camilla Parker Bowles.

★ Actor Jason Merrells, who plays Gavin Feraday in *Cutting It*, is the brother of actor Simon Merrells, who plays *Merseybeats'* Chris Traynor.

★ *Channel 4 News* presenter Jon Snow and *Tomorrow's World* presenter Peter Snow are cousins.

★ *Partridge Family* star and 70s pop singer David Cassidy's stepmother is actress Shirley Field.

★ Jennifer Aniston's godfather was Telly Savalas.

★ Soulful divas Whitney Houston and Dionne Warwick are cousins.

★ Poet laureate Cecil Day-Lewis was the father of actor Daniel Day-Lewis.

★ *Die Another Day* Bond villain Toby Stephens is the son of actors Sir Robert Stephens and Dame Maggie Smith.

★ *Dad's Army* star Bill Pertwee was the cousin of *Dr Who* actor Jon Pertwee, whose son is *Cold Feet* actor Sean Pertwee.

★ Jamie Lee Curtis is the daughter of *Psycho* actress Janet Leigh and movie star Tony Curtis.

★ ITV newsreader John Suchet and *Poirot* star David Suchet are brothers.

★ *Coupling* and *This Life* actor Jack Davenport is the nephew of disgraced former Tory MP Jonathan Aitken.

★ Chef Rick Stein is the uncle of Radio 1 presenter Judge Jules.

★ Ewan McGregor's uncle is *Holby City* actor Denis Lawson.

★ Loyd Grossman's father-in-law is *Chariots of Fire* producer Lord David Puttnam.

★ *EastEnders'* Laura Beale, actress Hannah Waterman, is the daughter of *Minder* star Dennis Waterman.

★ Aretha Franklin is Whitney Houston's godmother.

★ Hywel Bennett, who appeared as gangland boss Jack Dalton in *EastEnders*, is the brother of Alun Lewis, who played Vic Windsor in *Emmerdale*.

★ Former *Blue Peter* presenter Caron Keating is the daughter of fellow television presenter Gloria Hunniford.

★ American actors Charlie Sheen and Emilio Estevez are brothers. Their father is *West Wing* star Martin Sheen.

SECOND-CHOICE CELEBS

It's hard to imagine *Magnum* and *Three Men and a Baby* star Tom Selleck ever playing Indiana Jones. But if the film's producers had got their way, the tall, moustachioed one would have taken the role and Harrison Ford would never have got a look in.

And he's not the only one.

★ Whitney Houston's 1986 hit single 'How Will I Know?' was originally written for Janet Jackson's *Control* album, but Janet didn't like it, and so it was given to Whitney.

★ Ewan McGregor was offered the role of Neo in *The Matrix*. He turned it down and it eventually went to Keanu Reeves.

★ The American co-producers of David Attenborough's groundbreaking *Life on Earth* series originally wanted Robert Redford to present the programmes.

★ George Chakiris only won the lead male role in the Oscar-winning *West Side Story* after Elvis Presley turned down the part on the instruction of Colonel Tom Parker. Parker would not allow Presley to accept any role when he was not top of the bill.

★ Director John Huston did not initially consider the pairing of Sean Connery and Michael Caine, when casting *The Man Who Would Be King*. Huston had originally tried to persuade Clark Gable and Humphrey Bogart to play the two main parts, and when they declined he asked Paul Newman and Robert Redford to renew their acting partnership. Newman turned down the offer but suggested that Connery and Caine might be suitable for the roles.

★ Anita Dobson was not first choice to play Angie Watts in *EastEnders*. The role was initially given to unknown actress Jean Fennell, but she was sacked before the first episode.

★ In the 1930s actor Gary Cooper turned down what would become one of the most famous roles in movie history, when he said no to the part of Rhett Butler in *Gone with the Wind*. He declared the film was 'going to be the biggest flop in Hollywood history'. How wrong he was.

★ Another world-famous movie role was that of Dorothy in *The Wizard of Oz*. The part was originally intended for Shirley Temple, but when movie company MGM were unable to get her on loan from rival film company Fox, Judy Garland was cast in the role.

★ Before Roger Moore was cast as James Bond in *Live and Let Die*, Paul Newman, Robert Redford and Burt Reynolds were all considered for the part.

★ Sandra Bullock was only chosen to play the character of Annie in *Speed* after Halle Berry turned it down.

★ John Travolta only got the part of Vincent in the 1994 Quentin Tarantino cult classic *Pulp Fiction* because Tarantino's first choice, *Reservoir Dogs* star Michael Madsen, had other work commitments.

★ Canadian rocker Bryan Adams was not the first choice to perform the song 'Everything I do (I do it for you)' on the sound-track for the film *Robin Hood, Prince of Thieves*. Kate Bush, Annie Lennox and Lisa Stansfield turned down the ballad before Adams recorded it. The song went on to top the UK charts for a record sixteen weeks in 1991.

★ Tony Robinson only got the part of Baldrick in the

Blackadder series after Timothy Spall had turned it down.

★ Peter Bowles was first choice to play Jerry Leadbetter in the 70s comedy *The Good Life*, opposite Penelope Keith. Bowles said no to the role as he wanted to work in the theatre at the time, so Paul Eddington got the part. It was another four years before Bowles and Keith starred together in *To the Manor Born*.

★ Jodie Foster won the role of Clarice Starling in *Silence of the Lambs* only after Michelle Pfeiffer rejected it.

★ Meanwhile, co-star Anthony Hopkins only took the role of Hannibal Lecter in the same film after Gene Hackman had turned it down.

★ Glenn Close only got the lead role in *Fatal Attraction* after it was rejected by Debra Winger.

★ Gwyneth Paltrow's role in *Shakespeare in Love* was initially offered to Kate Winslet. Kate turned it down and Gwyneth went on to win the Best Actress Oscar for her performance in the film.

★ Richard Gere wasn't at the top of the producer's list when they were casting the role of Billy Flynn in the Oscar-winning film *Chicago*. John Travolta was initially offered the part, but turned it down after seeing the stage show, as he didn't believe it could be successfully translated to the big screen.

★ British-born actress Jane Leeves was not first choice to play Daphne in *Frasier*. The part was written with Lisa Maxwell in mind. Lisa, who appears in *The Bill*, talked herself out of the role after she annoyed the producers by criticising some of the lines in the script. Leeves went on to earn £240,000 an episode.

★ Lisa Stansfield turned down the role of the kooky bridesmaid in *Four Weddings and a Funeral*. The part went to Charlotte Coleman.

★ Woody Harrelson was not the first choice for the lead role in

Indecent Proposal. Both Charlie Sheen and John Cusack turned down the part. Cusack also turned down a starring role in *Apollo 13*.

★ Bing Crosby was the first choice to play the role of *Columbo*. Peter Falk eventually took the role of the detective with the trademark raincoat and cigar.

★ Cake-making actress Jane Asher wasn't first in the queue for the part of Angel Samson in the ill-fated revival of *Crossroads*. Former *Colby*'s actress Stephanie Beacham was offered the role, but turned it down on the grounds that it was 'not financially interesting enough'.

★ David Jason was the third choice to play Del Boy in *Only Fools and Horses*. Originally actor Enn Reital was given the part, while the second choice was *Iris* Oscar-winner Jim Broadbent, but both had other work commitments, so couldn't take the role.

★ Dustin Hoffman made his name opposite Anne Bancroft in *The Graduate*, but not before Robert Redford rejected the role of Benjamin Braddock.

★ The role of legendary Bond villain Ernst Stavros Blofeld in *You Only Live Twice* was meant to be played by a Czech actor called Jan Werich. It was only after Werich fell ill that Donald Pleasence was brought in at the last minute to take over the part.

★ Eddie Murphy was not first choice for the role of Axel Foley in *Beverly Hills Cop*, the film that was to be his big break. Producers wanted either Sylvester Stallone or Clint Eastwood to play the part.

★ Michael J Fox got his big break in films when he was cast as Marty McFly in *Back to the Future*. However, he was not first choice for the role. Eric Stolz was originally cast as the time-travelling teenager but was sacked after five weeks of filming.

★ Pete Postlethwaite was offered the chance to work with Martin Scorsese on the Oscar-nominated film *Gangs of New York*. However the star of *Romeo and Juliet* and *The Usual Suspects* was put off the project after discovering producers had convinced the cast to work for reduced pay, because 'everyone wants to work with Martin Scorsese'. Postlethwaite decided it was a bit of a scam and turned down the offer.

★ Jim Dale was second choice to play the lead role in the 1992 film *Carry On Columbus*. Robbie Coltrane, the first choice, turned down the part.

★ Harry Enfield also turned down a role in the film. He was annoyed that the *Carry On* brand had been resurrected after so many of the original cast had died.

★ Kevin Costner was originally offered the lead role of the American President in the 1997 film *Air Force One*. The part later went to Harrison Ford.

★ Meanwhile Harrison Ford was one of the actors initially considered for the part of Eliot Ness in *The Untouchables*. Mel Gibson was also considered, but it was Steven Spielberg who suggested Kevin Costner.

★ Nick Nolte was considered for the role of Han Solo in *Star Wars*.

★ Warren Beatty, Robert Redford, Paul Newman and James Caan were all considered for the role of *Superman* before Christopher Reeve.

★ Madonna was only given the role of Eva Peron in Alan Parker's film version of *Evita* because first choice, Michelle Pfeiffer, had just given birth to her second child and the producer's thought that she would find it difficult to cope with the demanding filming schedule in Britain, Argentina and Hungary.

★ Meanwhile Michelle Pfeiffer was a last-minute replacement for Madonna in the film *The Fabulous Baker Boys*, for which she earned an Oscar nomination.

★ Tom Hanks declined to play Kevin Spacey's role in *American Beauty* because of work commitments. Spacey went on to win the Best Actor Oscar for the film.

★ Gene Hackman was sixth choice to play Popeye Doyle in *The French Connection*. He won the Best Actor Oscar for the role in 1972.

★ Arthur Lowe was third choice for the role of Captain Mainwaring in the legendary sitcom *Dad's Army*. Both Thorley Walter and *Dr Who* actor Jon Pertwee had turned down the part.

★ Uma Thurman was not first choice to play Emma Peel in the 1998 film version of *The Avengers*. Gwyneth Paltrow had already declined the role.

★ Dame Judi Dench was not the first person to be cast as Jean in the BBC sitcom *As Time Goes By*. Actress Jean Simmons had accepted the part, but turned it down at the last minute after deciding to do a miniseries for American television instead.

★ John Travolta turned down the starring roles in *American Gigolo* and *An Officer and a Gentleman*. Richard Gere accepted both parts, and did very well out of them.

★ *X-Men* star Hugh Jackman was only cast as Wolverine after the original choice, Scottish actor Dougray Scott, had to drop out after shooting on *Mission Impossible 2* overran.

★ Anthony Hopkins was approached to play the role of Elliot Carver in the Bond film *Tomorrow Never Dies*, but after initial interest he turned down the part, which was eventually played by Jonathan Pryce.

★ Drew Barrymore was originally cast as Sidney Prescott in

the 1996 film *Scream*. However, due to schedule conflicts, she finally played the much smaller role of Casey Becker, with Neve Campbell taking the lead role.

★ George Segal was the preferred choice for the lead role in *10*. It was only given to Dudley Moore after Segal turned it down.

★ Elvis Presley was not the producer's first thought for the lead role of Clint Reno in *Love Me Tender*. Robert Wagner was originally considered for the part.

★ Michael Caine only got his acting break in *Zulu* after Roger Moore turned down the chance to play the young lieutenant who finds his contingent has been isolated.

★ Bette Midler turned down the role of Annie Wilkes in *Misery* because she thought it was the wrong part for her image. The part eventually went to Kathy Bates, who went on to win a Best Actress Oscar for her performance in the film.

★ Michael Crawford was not initially wanted for the role of Frank Spencer in *Some Mothers Do 'Ave 'Em*. Both Ronnie Barker and Norman Wisdom were asked to star in the show, but turned the offer down, while Crawford went on to create a comedy legend.

★ Lynda Bellingham was not the original choice for the lead role in the sitcom *Old Socks*. *Birds of a Feather* star Linda Robson was due to play the part, but had to pull out after suffering an acute attack of pancreatitis.

★ Meryl Streep was due to have starred in *Thelma and Louise* alongside Goldie Hawn before scheduling difficulties meant they both pulled out, leaving Susan Sarandon and Geena Davis to take on the roles.

OTHER CELEBRITY SETBACKS

The road to fame is not always an easy one. Some celebrities found that their early attempts to make it in their chosen field were thwarted before they had even begun. Others had to attend many auditions and face a great deal of rejection before they were finally given a chance to shine.

★ A BBC Scotland boss once told *GMTVs'* Lorraine Kelly that she would have to take elocution lessons if she wanted a career in broadcasting. She refused.

★ Comedian Jim Davidson failed the audition for the role of the Artful Dodger in the 1968 film version of *Oliver!* He was thirteen at the time.

★ When yachtswoman Ellen McArthur was ten, she came last in all the races at a sailing school, where most of the youngsters had better boats and equipment. On the journey home she decided that she would never let it happen again.

★ Tom Jones was once refused a recording contract because 'he sang too well and looked too masculine'.

★ Pierce Brosnan was originally cast as James Bond in 1986. Unfortunately for him, at the last minute his previously cancelled series *Remington Steele* was recommissioned. Brosnan was contractually obliged to stay with the programme, forcing him to give up the role of Bond, which eventually went to Timothy Dalton. It was not until 1995 that Brosnan got the chance to play 007 in *Goldeneye*.

★ Patsy Kensit auditioned for the role of Emily, Ross's fiancée, in *Friends*. She failed to impress the show's producers however, and the part eventually went to *Cold Feet*'s Helen Baxendale.

★ David Lynch, the director of *Blue Velvet*, was offered the chance to direct *Return of the Jedi*. He turned it down to make *Dune*, a film that flopped, while *Return of the Jedi* made millions.

★ Journalist and television presenter Matthew Wright says the BBC turned him down at least thirty times before he made his name in Fleet Street. This included a failed audition for Esther Rantzen's *That's Life!*

★ Ewan McGregor auditioned for the role of Romeo in Baz Luhrmann's production of the Shakespeare classic *Romeo and Juliet*. He didn't get the part, which went to Leonardo DiCaprio; however, Luhrmann remembered him and later cast him as the lead in his film *Moulin Rouge*.

★ Denise van Outen attended several auditions for the role of Sandy in the West End version of *Grease*, but was not given the role because at the time she was not considered famous enough. In an effort to change this, she moved into television presenting.

★ David Jason was hired and fired from *Dad's Army* in the same afternoon, because he was not famous enough. The show's writer David Croft cast Jason in the role of Corporal Jones, while at the same time the then BBC Head of Variety, Bill Cotton, was casting Clive Dunn for the part. When Croft told Cotton he had found an actor to play Corporal Jones, Cotton told him he had already found someone who was far better known, so Jason was dropped.

★ Jodie Foster failed to win the part of Princess Leia in *Star Wars* because she was considered too young – she was thirteen at the time.

★ *Sixth Sense* actor Haley Joel Osment was considered for the role of Harry Potter. It finally went to Daniel Radcliffe.

★ Elaine Lordan, who plays Lynne Slater in *EastEnders*, originally auditioned for the role of Nigel Bates's girlfriend Debbie. The part went to *Family Affair's* actress Nicola Duffet.

★ Gene Hackman failed to get the role of President Franklin Delano Roosevelt in *Pearl Harbor*. Jon Voight took the role.

★ Comedian Rik Mayall was cast in the role of the poltergeist Peeves in *Harry Potter and the Philosopher's Stone*. Unfortunately he ended up on the cutting-room floor and does not appear in the final edit of the film.

★ Also left on the cutting-room floor was singer David Essex, whose small role in *Carry On Henry* failed to make the final film.

★ Natalie Wood replaced *Hart to Hart* star Stefanie Powers in *West Side Story* because Powers was considered too young (she was fifteen at the time).

★ Former *Holby City* actress Lisa Faulkner admits she 'went to pieces' during auditions for the Bond movie *Die Another Day*. The role went to Halle Berry.

★ Former Spice Girl Emma Bunton faced early rejection when she failed the audition for the part of Bianca Jackson in *EastEnders*. The role went to Patsy Palmer.

★ Simon Webbe from Blue auditioned for the original series of *Popstars* but, in the middle of his auditioning performance, forgot the lyrics to the song he had chosen to sing. He didn't get through to the next round.

★ *Pearl Harbor* star Josh Hartnett auditioned six times for *Dawson's Creek*, but was never cast.

★ Before he scared the world as Freddy Krueger in *A*

Nightmare on Elm Street, actor Robert Englund auditioned for the role of Luke Skywalker in *Star Wars*. He failed to get the part, so persuaded his friend Mark Hamill to audition. Hamill won the role.

★ In 1993, while she was still appearing in *The Darling Buds of May*, Pete Waterman turned down Catherine Zeta Jones, when she asked him to help launch her pop career. He decided to offer the track he had written to Gayle and Gillian Blakeney, who were appearing in *Neighbours* at the time.

★ John Cleese had an early knock-back when the famous Cambridge Footlights revue rejected him, on the grounds that he couldn't sing or dance. He only managed to get in at a later date after collaborating with a friend on some comic sketches.

★ When she was eighteen, the BBC banned Welsh diva Shirley Bassey from performing 'Who Wants to Help me Burn the Candle at Both Ends' on the network because of the song's suggestive lyrics.

SPORTING CELEBRITIES

★ ★ ★ ★ ★ ★ ★ ★ ★ ★ ★ ★ ★ ★ ★ ★ ★ ★ ★ ★

This section is devoted to all things sport related. From personalities who showed great sporting talent when young, to sportsmen whose personalities have led to them becoming celebrities. Some may be old and bloated now, only getting any exercise when they walk to their chauffeur-driven limos, but once upon a time they were lean, mean, athletic machines (honest).

★ Rolf Harris was Australian Junior Backstroke Champion in 1946.

★ Actress Joely Richardson planned to be a professional tennis player and spent two years at a Florida tennis academy.

★ *Heartbeat* and *The Royal* actor Bill Maynard was on Leicester City's books until 'divided cruciates' ended his dreams of a footballing career.

★ In his youth, musical actor Darren Day was a semi-professional snooker player. His highest break was 136.

★ Paul Newman was the runner-up in the 1979 Le Mans endurance race and in 2003, at the age of 78, he finished second in another motor race.

★ Although he now looks as if he's enjoyed one too many 'barbies', *Home and Away's* Alf Stewart, actor Ray Meagher, was once a professional rugby football player.

★ *Poirot* actor David Suchet used to play rugby for Richmond RFC.

★ Legendary actor and comedian Bob Hope was a boxer in his

youth. He fought under the name of Packy East, and it is said that he won his first bout by hitting his opponent while he was looking the other way. He gave up the sport after getting knocked out in the ring.

★ *I'm a Celebrity...Get Me Out of Here* runner-up and England football player turned TV presenter John Fashanu, has a black belt in karate.

★ Irish actor Liam Neeson was also a professional boxer until he was seventeen. He was Youth Heavyweight Champion of Ireland several years running. His off-centre nose is the result of an early boxing injury.

★ American country music star Garth Brooks was noted for his football, baseball, basketball and track skills. However it was a javelin scholarship that got him into Oklahoma State University.

★ Before he was asking us 'Do You Think I'm Sexy?', Rod Stewart was an apprentice professional with Brentford Football Club. Still keen on the sport today, he has a full-size football pitch in the grounds of his British home.

★ Supermodel Jodie Kidd was an international show-jumper when she was thirteen and was chosen to represent England in the 2003 World Polo Championships.

★ The 'Muscles from Brussels', actor Jean-Claude Van Damme, once won the European Professional Karate Association middleweight championship.

★ *Royle Family* star Ricky Tomlinson was offered, but turned down, a trial for Scunthorpe United.

★ Former Monkee Davy Jones is a keen jockey and won his first major race at Lingfield in 1995 on the horse 'Big Race'.

★ Jonathan Dimbleby was the South of England show-jumping champion in 1964.

★ *Men in Black* star Tommy Lee Jones was once a champion polo player.

★ *Merseybeat* actress Haydn Gwynne represented her county at tennis.

★ *Buffy the Vampire Slayer*, a.k.a. Sarah Michelle Geller, was a competitive figure-skater for three years and was ranked third in the New York State regional competition.

★ David Frost once had a trial for Nottingham Forest FC.

★ Actor Hugh Laurie rowed in the 1980 University Boat Race.

★ Actor James Alexandrou, who plays Martin Fowler in *EastEnders*, used to swim for his county, and was once ranked in the top ten in the country for his age.

★ Former *Catchphrase* host Roy 'say what you see' Walker, was once the Northern Ireland hammer-throwing champion.

★ Despite having show business in his blood, Hollywood heart-throb George Clooney was set on a career in baseball. It was only when he failed a trial for the Cincinnati Reds that he turned to acting.

★ Chef Gordon Ramsey was signed by Glasgow Rangers at the age of fifteen, but left the squad to go to catering college.

★ Actor Richard Gere won a gymnastics scholarship to Massachusetts University.

★ *Dirty Dancing* and *Ghost* star Patrick Swayze also went to university on a gymnastics scholarship, as well as spending time at two of America's top ballet schools. He gave up dancing for a time after being bullied for it, but later returned, only finally giving it up for good when a knee injury proved too serious.

★ Football presenter Gabby Logan represented Wales in the rhythmic gymnastics team in the 1990 Commonwealth Games.

★ Actor Burt Reynolds won a football scholarship to Florida State University in the 1950s. He was set on a career as a halfback until he was involved in a car accident, which ended his sporting dreams and led to him turning his attentions to acting.

★ *Friends* star Matthew Perry was a top-ranked junior tennis player in Canada.

★ Singer Julio Iglesias started his career as a goalkeeper for Real Madrid. His career was cut short by a serious car accident in 1963. While recovering in hospital, one of the nurses gave him a guitar.

★ Television and radio presenter James Whale was the 1965 Surrey Junior Archery Champion.

★ Football commentator and former *It's a Knockout* host Stuart Hall played for Crystal Palace reserves in 1953.

★ Singer Alicia Keys is an excellent swimmer and actually trained for the Olympics.

★ Angus Deayton was given a football trial for Crystal Palace when he was twelve.

★ Film legend Kirk Douglas was once a professional wrestler.

★ Not content with winning five Olympic gold medals for rowing, Sir Steve Redgrave was also a member of the 1989–90 British bobsleigh team.

★ When he was controller of BBC2 in the late '60s, Sir David Attenborough was responsible for getting snooker on television.

★ *Ready Steady Cook* presenter Ainsley Harriott was once a ball boy at Wimbledon.

★ Comedian Jim Davidson (Bournemouth 1981–82), Jasper Carrott (Birmingham City 1979–82), snooker player Steve Davis

(Leyton Orient), and Sir Richard Attenborough (Chelsea 1969–82) have all been directors of football clubs.

★ Spoon-bender Uri Geller is co-chairman of Exeter City Football Club. Michael Jackson is an honorary director of the club.

★ Footballer Bobby Charlton scored 49 goals in 106 international games, making him England's all-time leading goal scorer.

★ Boxer Frank Bruno is said to have turned down a role in *Rocky V* because he thought it would be too embarrassing to get knocked down by Sylvester Stallone.

★ Only three people have won the BBC Sports Personality of the Year award twice: Henry Cooper (1967 and 1970), Nigel Mansell (1986 and 1992) and Damon Hill (1994 and 1996).

★ Pelé learned to play football by kicking a ball made of old socks around the streets of his home town.

★ Ian Botham once played football for Scunthorpe United. He was also the Somerset under-16 badminton doubles champion.

★ Australian cricketing legend Shane Warne only drifted into the game after failing to fulfil his dream of a career in Aussie rules football.

★ No stranger to getting in trouble, Warne was once caught smoking on camera while in the middle of a promotional advertising contract for Nicorette Chewing Gum.

★ In the late 70s footballer-turned-pundit Andy Gray owned a nightclub called the Holy City Zoo in Birmingham. Boy George once won a competition there for being the 'Weirdest-looking Person in the North'.

★ Eddie Irvine's parents were going to christen him Stirling Moss Irvine and only changed their mind at the last minute.

★ As a young player, David Ginola trained at a special football centre in Nice. However he was dropped after the coaches decided he was too thin. His skeletal appearance earned him the nickname *Jambes des Baguettes*, or 'Breadstick Legs'!

★ You can study David Beckham as part of a twelve- week 'football culture' module for a degree course at Staffordshire University.

★ Tennis player Anna Kournikova collects dolls from every country she visits.

★ Golfer Seve Ballesteros has such big hands he can hold eleven golf balls at the same time.

★ Model Jordan once revealed that former Manchester United player Dwight Yorke, with whom she had a relationship, used to wind up manager Sir Alex Ferguson by ostentatiously chewing gum while sitting on the subs' bench.

★ Former Formula One world champion Damon Hill was reluctant to get into a car, until his mother paid for him to attend a racing school in France at the age of 23. Until that point he had been racing motorbikes.

★ Sven Goran Eriksson uses Tibetan poetry to relax.

CELEBRITIES WHO HAVE A TWIN

They say that everybody has a twin or doppelgänger somewhere out there. But in the case of these celebrities, they really do.

Keith Chegwin (twin brother Jeff)

Jerry Hall (twin sister Terry)

Alanis Morrisette (twin brother Wade)

Kiefer Sutherland (twin sister Rachel)

Justin Timberlake (twin sister Laura died when still a baby)

Lowri Turner (twin sister Catrin)

Will Young (twin brother Rupert)

FACTS ABOUT FAMOUS MUSICAL
PERFORMERS

Their music provides the soundtrack to our lives, and the words of their songs often tell tales of love, betrayal and heartache. But what do we know about the real lives of those we see every week on *Top of the Pops*?

Here are some things you may not have heard them singing about.

★ Kylie (as in Minogue) is Aborigine for 'Boomerang'.

★ Early in his career, Canadian rocker Bryan Adams was lead singer of a band called Sweeney Todd. He recorded several songs for them before leaving the band in 1977. On those recordings, his voice was speeded up so it didn't sound so raspy.

★ U2 guitarist 'The Edge' got his nickname from singer Bono because of his 'sharp mind'.

★ Bono wrote the song 'The Sweetest Thing' after missing his wife's birthday. When the song was rerecorded, his wife, Ali Hewson, received all the proceeds of its sale. She gave them to charity.

★ Abba were originally known as the Hootenanny Singers.

★ Both Texas and Travis took their names from the 1984 Wim Wenders film *Paris, Texas*. Travis was the name of the main character.

★ The members of the group that was to become U2 began

their musical careers playing Rolling Stones and Beach Boys cover versions in a group called Feedback.

★ Mariah Carey got her big break thanks to a friend who pushed a demo cassette into the hands of Sony Music's president Tommy Mottola at a showbiz party. While driving home from the party Mottola played the cassette in the car and was so impressed that he immediately set out to track Carey down.

★ Charlotte Church is the youngest artist to enter the classical charts at Number One. She was just twelve years old when her *Voice of an Angel* CD hit the top spot in 1998.

★ While working as an advertising copy clerk, David Bowie wrote to washing-machine millionaire John Bloom, asking him for support and financial backing. Bloom agreed to hire Bowie to play at his wedding anniversary ball. However, after just two songs, Bloom had Bowie removed from the stage.

★ The father of Fatboy Slim, a.k.a. Norman Cook, introduced the bottle bank to Britain, and was later honoured by the Queen for his achievement.

★ While pregnant with her son Rocco, Madonna craved Cumbrian baker Jean Johnson's sticky toffee puddings. She was reported to have had regular deliveries of the dessert flown 5,000 miles to her Los Angeles home.

★ Despite never owning a teddy bear as a child, Meat Loaf has collected stuffed toys for over thirty years. The first one he bought was a raccoon in New York.

★ DJ Paul Oakenfold trained as a chef before being introduced to decks in the early 80s.

★ Fellow cool DJ Carl Cox used to perform at weddings.

★ Sinead O'Connor's only number-one record, 'Nothing

Compares 2 U', was actually written by fellow musician Prince. The song was originally recorded by Prince's protégés The Family, but failed to make an impression in the British chart.

★ Whitney Houston originally wanted to become a vet before she started singing.

★ Tom Jones used to wear his tuxedo trousers so tight that they had to have double seams.

★ Britney Spears is said to warn all concert promoters that if she receives any unwanted calls in her dressing room before a show they will be fined £3,000.

★ Damon Albarn from Blur named his daughter Missy, after Missy Elliott.

★ Before she was a Sugababe, Heidi Range was in an early incarnation of Atomic Kitten.

★ Jennifer Lopez employs a bottom make-up artist, as well as a coat-holder.

★ Depeche Mode took their name from the title of a French fashion magazine that was seen by lead singer Dave Gahan. The name translated means 'fast fashion'.

★ As a child, Shania Twain's parents used to wake her up in the middle of the night so she could perform at after-hours clubs. By the age of eight she had performed at most of the venues in her area.

★ Michael Jackson, whose album *Thriller* remains the world's biggest-selling album ever, has admitted that he doesn't like pop music.

★ David Essex is of Romany descent and is patron of the Gypsy Council, which helps protect the rights of travellers in the UK.

★ George Michael and Wham! partner Andrew Ridgeley once

turned down the chance to play waiters in US police series *Miami Vice*.

★ Dannii Minogue had her own fan club by the age of twelve.

★ One of Elvis's favourite night-time hobbies was visiting the Memphis morgue to look at corpses.

★ In the 70s clean-living family boy band The Osmonds had their single 'Crazy Horses' banned in South Africa, because government authorities believed the song was a eulogy to heroin.

★ Jon Bon Jovi turned down the lead role in the dance movie *Footloose* in order to concentrate on music.

★ Sting wrote his Grammy-winning song 'Every Breath You Take' sitting at Noel Coward's piano, while staying at Bond creator Ian Fleming's 'Goldeneye' house in the Caribbean.

★ Celine Dion's son's baptism on 25 July 2001 was broadcast live throughout Canada.

★ Beach Boy Brian Wilson's dad was said to be a tyrant who enjoyed scaring Brian by taking out his glass eye to reveal an empty socket.

★ S Club 7's hit song 'Reach', Kylie's award-winning 'Can't Get You Out Of My Head' and Will Young's record-breaking 'Anything Is Possible' were all written by 90s pop star Cathy Dennis.

★ The Manic Street Preachers decided upon the name for their band when a passer-by shouted it out to singer James Dean Bradfield while he was out busking.

★ Ms Dynamite lived in a hostel after moving out of the family home when she was still at school, but continued with her studies.

★ Soul star Solomon Burke has 21 children. When not performing, Burke runs a chain of funeral parlours in America.

★ Cher only began working as a session singer in an effort to finance an acting career.

★ The Bee Gees had six stamps issued in their honour by the Isle of Man in 1999. Their mother had run a local post office on the island, where the Gibb brothers were born.

★ Elton John received £350,000 from the *Sunday Mirror* in 1993, after they printed an article about him alleging that he was suffering from eating disorders.

★ Gareth Gates is scared of bats.

★ Jennifer Lopez originally trained to be a lawyer.

★ American rockers Aerosmith reportedly once asked their record company to pay royalty cheques directly to their drug dealers. Record bosses complained.

★ Andy McCluskey, who enjoyed several hits as part of 80s band Orchestral Manoeuvres in the Dark, was the mastermind behind Atomic Kitten.

★ Atomic Kitten were originally going to be called Automatic Kittens.

★ MTV used 55 cameras to record the daily lives of *The Osbournes* during the filming of the hit docu-soap.

★ Jamiroquai front man Jay Kay used to be a break-dancer.

★ Before embarking on a musical career, Billy Joel was a boxer. He retired after 25 fights and 21 victories, when he was knocked out and suffered a broken nose.

★ Westlife were barred from playing Ireland's premier venue Slane Castle because the owner, Lord Henry Mountcharles, didn't like boy bands. He reportedly said at the time, 'I have no time for manufactured groups.'

★ Prince has a phobia about dirt.

★ In January 1996, Samantha Fox was banned from singing at

a charity concert in Calcutta because of police fears that she might start a riot.

★ Sinead O'Connor has been ordained as a Catholic priest with the name Mother Bernadette Marie O'Connor.

★ Geri Halliwell, Robbie Williams, Kylie Minogue and *Pop Idol* judge Simon Cowell have all appeared in comic strips in the *Beano*.

★ Janet Jackson appeared in the US sitcom *Diff'rent Strokes* during the early 80s. She played the part of Willis's girlfriend.

★ Bart Simpson's hit single 'Do the Bartman', was anonymously written by Michael Jackson.

★ In 1966 the Beatles were forced to flee Manila in the Philippines, after refusing to have tea with the president's wife, Imelda Marcos.

★ George Harrison recommended the Rolling Stones to Decca records A&R man Dick Rowe and said he should sign them. Rowe had famously turned down the Beatles, but he didn't make the same mistake twice.

★ Geri Halliwell is said to go through the same superstitious ritual every time she releases a record – she closes all the toilet lids in her house.

★ Victoria Beckham is terrified of outer space but says that Beatrix Potter books calm her down.

★ Elton John plays the piano on the Hollies classic 'He Ain't Heavy, He's My Brother'.

★ Russian duo Tatu was originally known as 'Taty' when they first formed and rose to fame in their home country. The name is said to be a play on the phrase *ta lyubit tu*, which translates as 'she loves her'.

★ Wild man of rock, Alice Cooper, admitted that he drank a whole bottle of whisky to control his nerves, the first time he used a boa constrictor as a prop on stage.

★ Just before U2 went into the studio to record their album *October*, Bono lost all the lyrics to the new songs, and had to sing them from memory.

★ Noddy Holder wrote the tune to 'Merry Xmas Everybody' in 1967, six years before the song was first released. It was the first song he had ever written, but originally did not have festive lyrics.

★ Posters of Jennifer Lopez wearing just a skimpy flesh-coloured outfit were banned in Canada after causing chaos as drivers gawped at her picture. The posters were promoting her film *The Cell*.

★ Twiggy appeared on *This Is Your Life* at the age of just twenty.

★ Charlotte Church turned down a role in the movie version of Andrew Lloyd Webber's *Phantom Of The Opera* – because the filmmakers wanted her to lose weight.

★ Kylie Minogue, Blur, Madonna and Coldplay front man Chris Martin are all big fans of the board game Scrabble. Fellow musician Moby is also such a fan that he has even printed out his own list of allowable two-letter words.

★ Kylie Minogue once worked in a video-rental shop.

★ Debbie Harry is said to have named her band Blondie after the constant shouts of passing truck drivers when they saw her on the street.

★ George Michael's 1987 hit 'I Want Your Sex' was banned from daytime radio in the UK.

★ Adam Faith discovered 70s big-haired singer Leo Sayer.

★ Musical composer Sir Tim Rice features on the backing vocal of the Scaffold song 'Lily the Pink'. He wrote 'It's Easy For You', the last song on the last album that Elvis Presley ever recorded. He also wrote 'The Only Way To Go' which was the last track on the last album that Bing Crosby ever recorded.

★ Gareth Gates's first television appearance was on Michael Barrymore's *My Kind of People* in 1995, when he was just eleven years old. He was seen performing in the Meadowhall Centre in Sheffield.

★ Sheryl Crow once toured with Michael Jackson as a backing singer.

★ John Lennon's 'Starting Over' was Britain's first-ever posthumous Christmas Number One.

★ Joe Dolce's 1981 novelty record 'Shaddap You Face' was recorded in 35 different languages.

★ Country singing legend Willie Nelson once queued up at the Glastonbury Festival to get Rolf Harris's autograph. Harris thought he was a Willie Nelson lookalike.

★ *Pop Idol* runner-up Darius Danesh was named after a Persian king.

★ David Bowie was the first rock star to float himself on the stock exchange.

★ P Diddy has admitted he is scared of the dark.

★ Elton John once entered a song in the contest to find Britain's entry for the Eurovision Song Contest. Unfortunately 'I've Been Loving You Too Long' failed to win the competition, and Lulu performed 'Boom Bang-a-Bang' instead.

★ Beach Boy Dennis Wilson was the only member of the band who actually surfed.

★ Ozzy Osbourne has been into rehab fourteen times.

★ *Pop Idol* reject Rik Waller does not have any qualifications, having left school when he was just fifteen.

★ Rick Parfitt from Status Quo decided to liven up one of the band's *Top of the Pops* performances in the 1980s by walking into the drum kit and falling over. He claims he wasn't drunk at the time.

★ Aretha Franklin's voice has been designated a natural resource by the state of Michigan.

★ In 1970 Julio Iglesias lost out to Dana in the Eurovision Song Contest. He represented Spain with the song 'Gwendolyn'.

★ When he was a child, Noel Gallagher was nicknamed 'Brezhnev', because of his distinctive bushy eyebrows.

★ James Brown was often known as being a hard man to work for. He would fine his band members if their shoes were not properly shined, or if they missed a note.

★ Bangles' member Susanna Hoffs wrote the Atomic Kitten hit 'Love Doesn't Have To Hurt'.

★ Justin Timberlake's mum came up with the name of Justin's group N'SYNC, by taking the last letter of each of the band member's Christian names.

★ Before joining Eurovision-winners Bucks Fizz, Cheryl Baker was a member of the group 'Co-Co', which represented Britain in the 1978 Eurovision Song Contest.

★ Dido was born on Christmas Day, but has adopted 25 June as her official birthday, borrowing the date from Paddington Bear.

★ Legendary Queen guitarist Brian May perfected his technique by buying records and copying the most complicated guitar parts.

★ Former All Saint Nicole Appleton appeared in *Santa Claus The Movie*.

★ Her sister Natalie has a tattoo of a dagger plunging between her vertebrae and coming out again. She says it is a reference to people stabbing her in the back.

★ Tracy Chapman rose to fame after returning to the stage during Nelson Mandela's seventieth-birthday concert, when Stevie Wonder's backing tapes went missing.

★ Cliff Richard's 1959 film *Serious Charge* was banned in some areas as it dealt with the then controversial subject of blackmailing homosexuals.

★ Elton John started having piano lessons when he was four years old.

★ Bee Gee Robin Gibb is fascinated with the occult. He bought his wife a Jaguar with the number plate DRUID, as she is patroness of the Druids.

★ Actor Macaulay Culkin had to teach Marilyn Manson how to smoke during the filming of *Party Monster*, in which they appeared together, as Manson didn't know how to.

★ Rolling Stone Keith Richard sang in the choir at the coronation of Queen Elizabeth II.

★ Before she enjoyed her own chart success, Martine McCutcheon appeared in an Enya video.

★ Christina Aguilera was eight when she made her first professional appearance on the nationally syndicated American *Star Search* show. Aguilera's voice range is four octaves.

★ Rock legends Led Zeppelin got their name thanks to Who drummer Keith Moon. Moon was originally offered the chance to be drummer in the band, before John Bonham got the gig. Moon turned the offer down, however, declaring that the band would 'go down like a lead zeppelin'.

★ In the early 50s, Tom Jones spent more than a year in bed while suffering from tuberculosis.

★ When he formed his band in 1978, Jarvis Cocker named it Arabicus Pulp, after reading an article in the *Financial Times* about the coffee trade during an economics class. They later shortened the name to Pulp.

★ Jon Bon Jovi's first recording experience was singing the song 'R2-D2 we wish you a merry Christmas' on a *Star Wars* Christmas Album, *Christmas with the Stars*, which was produced by his cousin.

★ Elton John's uncle was a professional soccer player. He broke his leg playing for Nottingham Forest in the 1959 FA Cup Final.

★ Frank Sinatra once suggested that he and Tom Jones go into business together and buy a Las Vegas hotel. Tom's son is believed to have blocked the idea.

★ Barry White's records have been used by marine biologists to help encourage sharks to make love.

★ Even though former choirboy Aled Jones is most famous for singing 'Walking In The Air' from *The Snowman*, his voice doesn't appear on the original film soundtrack.

★ Britney Spears is a Baptist, and reportedly keeps a 'Bible Book' in which she writes down her daily prayers.

★ Alice Cooper was a good friend and admirer of Groucho Marx. When the legendary comedian died, he bought one of the 'O's from the famous 'HOLLYWOOD' sign and dedicated it to his memory.

★ Although his Cockney accent is part of his singing style, Madness front man Suggs was actually born in Hastings and only moved to London as a child.

★ Moby refuses to travel anywhere by car because of the harm they do the environment.

★ Tom Jones was on Charles Manson's hit list. He had been renting a house opposite Sharon Tate when she was murdered and when the police raided Manson's house they reportedly found the list.

★ Holly Valance was modelling from the age of four and bought her own house at the age of sixteen.

★ In 1954 Jim Denny, the manager of the Grand Old Opry in Tennessee, told Elvis Presley, 'You ain't going nowhere, son. You ought to go back to driving a truck.' Elvis didn't take his advice.

★ Country star Willie Nelson wrote the song 'Bring Me Sunshine', which was to become Morecambe and Wise's unofficial theme tune.

★ Madonna was once two hours late for a gala dinner hosted by Prince Charles. The reason for her tardiness – she couldn't decide which outfit to wear.

★ Shaggy was once a US Marine, serving in the Gulf War of 1991.

★ Gloria Estefan once asked Mariah Carey to write a song for her for a film, and Mariah agreed. However, after she'd written it, her then husband Tommy Mottola, president of Sony Music, changed Mariah's mind and told her to keep it for herself.

★ Beatle Ringo Starr opened a furniture company in the early 1970s, which sold coffee tables made from Rolls-Royce grills.

★ Dido's family didn't own a television when she was growing up, so she spent her teenage years listening to her brother's record collection and playing with a classical orchestra.

★ Kylie Minogue was the first female singer to have all of her first thirteen singles reach the UK top ten.

★ Christina Aguilera's surname is Spanish for 'eagle's nest'.

★ American soul singer Luther Vandross sang backing vocals on David Bowie's hit 'Young Americans', and also co-wrote Bowie's hit single 'Fame'.

★ Rod Stewart was the first rock star to have a concert broadcast worldwide by satellite, during a performance in 1981.

★ US interrogators in Baghdad used heavy-metal songs by Metallica to break Iraqi captives, following the 2003 war on Iraq. Officials said that subjecting prisoners to long sessions of the 'culturally offensive' music encouraged them to talk. The interrogators favourite Metallica track was 'Enter Sandman', which contained the lyric 'Sleep with one eye open, gripping your pillow tight'.

★ Jay Kay named his band Jamiroquai after an Iroquois tribe that inspired him.

★ Who guitarist Pete Townshend accidentally broke the neck of his guitar while swinging it around at a venue that had a low ceiling. The audience enjoyed it so much that it became a regular feature of the act.

★ When Craig David was fifteen, his mother encouraged him to enter a song-writing competition to write a B-side for the boy band Damage. He won and the song appeared on the B-side of 'Wonderful Tonight', which got to number three in the charts in 1997.

★ Singer Belinda Carlisle had 32 stalkers at one point in her career, and had to wear a bulletproof vest on stage.

★ Ms Dynamite is the eldest of eleven children.

★ Celine Dion, meanwhile, is the youngest of fourteen children. Dion's dressing room for her three-year Caesars Palace residency in Las Vegas, covers 2,400 square feet. Among its features are a massage room, a £3 million 3D video screen complete with sound system, and a £1.4 million cooling system that is meant to protect her vocal chords from the dry Nevada climate.

★ Dusty Springfield was the only female performer to appear on *Top of the Pops* when it first transmitted in January 1964.

★ Tina Turner made her 1980s comeback with the help of two former members of The Human League. After asking her to record a track with them, Martyn Ware and Ian Craig Marsh went on to produce her cover of Al Green's 'Let's Stay Together'.

★ Before becoming the nation's *Pop Idol*, Will Young took part in a *This Morning* competition to find a new boy band. He won, but nothing came of it.

★ Charlotte Church sang at *Pop Idol* judge Nicki Chapman's wedding.

★ Robbie Williams is a big fan of board games. He is said to be especially good at draughts, as well as Uno and chess.

★ The Shadows represented Britain in the 1975 Eurovision Song Contest with the song 'Let Me Be The One'. On the night, band member Bruce Welch forgot the words and fluffed the first line, but the group still finished second in the contest.

★ John Lennon gave his last autograph to Mark David Chapman – the man who shot him.

★ Dolly Parton's song 'I Will Always Love You' is the most requested song at UK funerals.

★ Whitney Houston used to be a backing singer for Chaka Khan.

★ Although the soundtrack to *Saturday Night Fever* is one of the best-selling soundtracks of all time, Robin Gibb has admitted that he is a poor dancer and doesn't think any of the

Bee Gees have ever been to a disco.

★ Uri Geller once designed an album cover for Belinda Carlisle.

★ Pink allegedly got her nickname not from her hair colour, but from the colour she turned after having her pants pulled down when she was at school.

★ Donny Osmond, 70s pin-up, is a qualified electrical engineer. He oversaw the wiring of the Osmond's production studio in their home state of Utah.

★ Kylie Minogue's *Live in Sydney* DVD and her book *Kylie: Naked* have been banned in Malaysia for showing too much flesh.

★ Dannii Minogue's single 'Who Do You Love Now?' has actually sold more copies worldwide than sister Kylie's much-celebrated record 'Can't Get You Out Of My Head'.

★ Singing legend Nat 'King' Cole started his career as a jazz pianist, and didn't believe his voice was very good. He had to be talked into stepping in front of the microphone. Cole once had a television show cancelled because of hostility from the show's sponsors Max Factor. They complained that they couldn't sell their lipsticks on a show that was presented by a black man.

★ Oasis front man Liam Gallagher suffers badly from hay fever, and has also suffered from agoraphobia.

★ The Spice Girls were originally going to be called 'Touch'.

★ Columbian singer Shakira left her family home when she was just thirteen to pursue a modelling career. She ended up signing a recording contract, but when her debut album failed to be a success, she returned to high school.

★ Damon Albarn met future Blur bandmate Graham Coxon when he was twelve years old. Their first band name was 'Two's a Crowd'.

★ Actor Johnny Depp played guitar on the 1997 Oasis album *Be Here Now*.

★ Dolly Parton once entered a Dolly Parton lookalike competition and failed to win.

★ Jennifer Lopez is known as 'The Supernova' in the Bronx, and has also been nicknamed 'La Guitarra', because her shapely curves are said to resemble those of a guitar. Lopez used to take the Number 6 train from her home in the Bronx to get to auditions in Manhattan. The experience was her inspiration for the title of her debut album *On the 6*.

★ Stevie Wonder was blinded at birth when too much oxygen was administered while he was in an incubator.

★ Boy George paid £42,000 in 1983 to appear as himself as a kidnap victim in the American action series *The A Team*.

★ Glam rocker from the 70s Alvin Stardust decided to dye his hair jet black for his first *Top of the Pops* performance. Unfortunately the dye left Alvin with huge black streaks running down his face that he couldn't wash off. In desperation he asked an expert in fake face hair to help him sculpt a pair of massive sideburns to wear on stage. The look was such a hit that he had to maintain the facial hair.

★ Paul McCartney and John Lennon first met at a fete at St Peter's Parish Church in Woolton on 6 July 1957. Ivan Vaughan introduced them.

★ George Harrison once owned a toilet that played 'Lucy in the Sky with Diamonds'.

★ Cher was diagnosed with dyslexia at the age of thirty.

★ Ozzy Osbourne may be worth £85 million nowadays, but his family's fortunes weren't always so great. As a child, his parents used to put a can of soup in a saucepan of water to make it go further.

★ Former Monkee Mickey Dolenz produced the ITV children's series *Metal Mickey*.

★ Fellow Monkee Peter Tork paid $160,000 in 1968 to be released from his Monkees contract. It was reported that other members of the band also wanted to leave, but were put off by the amount such a split would cost them. They eventually disbanded in 1970.

★ Stereophonics were the first band to be signed by Richard Branson's V2 records.

★ Britney Spears needed four stitches after a heavy camera fell on her during the filming of the video for 'Oops! I Did It Again'.

★ Celine Dion's first name comes from a song – 'Celine', sung by Hugues Aufray – that her mother was singing while she was pregnant.

★ Debbie Harry and Blondie were originally asked to record the theme song to the James Bond film *For Your Eyes Only*. However when they heard it, the film company didn't like it and asked them to rerecord the track. When they refused, Sheena Easton was brought in to record an alternative song.

★ Robbie Williams had just thirty minutes' worth of horse-riding lessons before he appeared as a cowboy in the video to 'Feel'.

★ Monkee Mike Nesmith's mum made $47 million when she sold the patent for liquid paper in 1979. She died the following year and left all her money to Mike.

★ In 1983, *Billboard* magazine declared that Madonna was simply 'a flash in the pan'.

★ Elton John wrote 'Song For Guy' as a tribute to a

Rocket Records motorcycle messenger who was killed in a road accident.

★ It was at a concert in Minneapolis in 1954 that Al Dvorin first closed Elvis's concert with the words, 'Ladies and Gentlemen, Elvis has left the building. Thank you and good night.'

★ Elvis's mother and father both had bit parts in his film *Loving You*.

★ In 1996, when Oasis played at Knebworth in front of 250,000 people, 5 per cent of the UK population applied for a ticket.

★ Peter Gabriel wrote the music for the Millennium Dome show. It was later released as the album *Ovo*.

★ Bob Marley's dad was an English army captain.

★ Before making it big as a singer, Anastacia made regular appearances as a dancer on MTV's *Club MTV* as well featuring in a couple of videos for Salt-N-Pepa.

★ Legendary producer Phil Spector was a perfectionist in the recording studios. Once, when working with Leonard Cohen, he held a gun to the singer's head to get the performance he wanted.

★ Blur drummer Dave Rowntree's father was the sound engineer for the Beatles at the BBC.

★ Madonna used to play the drums in a band.

★ Simon and Garfunkel's song 'Cecilia' was banned in Malawi in the 1970s because it was also the name of the mistress of the country's then leader, President Banda.

★ *Fame Academy* winner David Sneddon was given the lead part in a West End show co-produced by Adam Faith when he was eighteen. The show collapsed, however, because the writer, director, and producer fell out over a legal matter.

★ Frank Sinatra's management used to pay girls to scream at the crooner as he performed on stage.

★ Eric Clapton sang backing vocals on The Beatles hit 'All You Need Is Love'.

★ Luciano Pavarotti once called Bono's father relentlessly, so that he would try to convince his son to write a song for him.

★ Fatboy Slim collects 'Acieeed' smiley face ephemera.

★ When Christina Aguilera attended her senior prom with her boyfriend, her envious classmates walked off the dance floor when her song 'Genie In A Bottle' played.

★ MC Hammer, who was topping the charts in the early 1990s with songs such as 'U Can't Touch This', had to work as a telephone salesman after being declared bankrupt in 1996 with debts of more than $10 million. The debts had accrued despite the fact that Hammer had earned $33 million in 1990 and 1991.

★ Queen guitarist Brian May built his first guitar when he was sixteen. He made it from an old fireplace and used shelf-edging to emboss it.

★ George Michael claims he was watching *Match of the Day* when he wrote the worldwide hit song 'Careless Whisper'.

★ Keith Richard suffered a near-fatal electrocution while on stage in 1965. The rubber soles of his Hush Puppies reportedly saved him.

★ Celine Dion collects shoes and is said to own over 600 pairs.

★ Otis Redding, John Denver, Patsy Cline and Buddy Holly all died in plane crashes.

★ Singing sisters The Nolans sold over nine million records in Japan, which means that one in every four Japanese households owned a Nolans LP.

★ Ms Dynamite got her stage name when a friend pulled it out of a hat.

★ Bono reportedly once paid £1,000 to have his favourite trilby flown first class to Italy from West London, so he could wear it during a charity concert. Even though the hat had its own first-class seat, flight attendants were so concerned that it would either get squashed or go missing that they moved it into the cockpit.

★ Easy listening maestro Andy Williams is so conscious of his lack of height that he has always insisted on being shot by a low camera, while ensuring that he always sits on the tallest stool for any interviews or duets.

★ Paul McCartney wrote 'When I'm Sixty-Four' when he was fifteen.

★ Ozzy Osbourne is dyslexic.

DEMANDING DIVAS

As well as commanding fees so high they make some members of the Royal Family appear only 'quite well off', many pop stars and actors make other demands to record companies and film executives, and often refuse to perform if their wishes are not met.

But who are the worst offenders?

★ Known for her diva-like behaviour, Jennifer Lopez once arrived at the *Top of the Pops* studios with an entourage of eighteen, demanded that her ten dressing rooms should be decorated only in white and that they should be filled with the finest lilies.

★ While staying at the Metropolitan hotel in London, Lopez ordered a fleet of six Mercedes cars to take her and her companions the 200 yards between her hotel and the Dorchester, where she was having lunch.

★ It is also rumoured that she has given instructions that her coffee must only be stirred in an anti-clockwise direction.

★ Sylvester Stallone refused to promote his film *Demolition Man* until the room his press interviews were to take place in was painted peach. He didn't like the original yellow colour.

★ Actress Kim Basinger always insists on only washing her hair with mineral water.

★ Cher is also renowned for making excessive backstage

demands. According to popular rumour, she insists on a separate dressing room for her wigs.

★ Mariah Carey has been known to ask for a selection of 'live' puppy dogs in her room to play with.

★ Carey also once ordered shop assistants to completely redecorate a shop toilet because she wanted to use it, and caused a mile-long traffic jam in London when she got her limousine driver to stop in the middle of the city so she could touch up her make-up prior to a radio interview.

★ Wild men of rock, Aerosmith, had a reputation for excessive demands at the height of their fame. Noddy Holder from Slade, who supported the band on several occasions, has recounted events during one concert in which the concert promoter was sent out for white towels late into the evening, because the band didn't like the colour of the towels they had been given.

★ Fellow rocker Eddie Van Halen also demonstrated diva-like behaviour by insisting that the bowls of M&M sweets in his dressing room did not contain any brown ones.

★ When Jim Carrey was filming *Ace Ventura: When Nature Calls*, he demanded two personal chefs. One was to cook for him, the other was to cater for his pet iguana.

★ Elton John insists that the temperature of his dressing room must be 60 degrees in summer and 70 degrees in winter.

★ Martine McCutcheon showed signs of diva behaviour when she made a list of demands before appearing on *The Frank Skinner Show*. She allegedly requested Laurent-Perrier pink champagne, twelve bottles of water at room temperature, grilled chicken, fruit, and red and white roses.

★ Mary J Blige reportedly demands that the first $100,000 of her fee be paid on the night in $100 bills.

★ Whitney Houston once held up a video shoot for over four hours, simply because she didn't like the chair in her dressing room.

★ Before she gets into a bath, one of Houston's assistants always has to check the water to make sure it isn't too cold or too hot.

★ Actress Demi Moore not only demanded a $5 million pay cheque to appear in the 1994 film *Disclosure*, but also a double-sized trailer, with a lawn and a forest of fig trees outside.

★ The members of Destiny's Child always refuse to drink from cups made from plastic or Styrofoam.

★ Security-conscious Shania Twain has requested sniffer dogs at certain venues to sniff out bombs.

★ Among P Diddy's excessive dressing-room demands are 264 towels and 24 bars of soap.

★ Britney Spears has a rather sweeter request – a supply of Gummie Bear soft sweets. Meanwhile, while she is on tour, she has her favourite coffee flown in by helicopter from the Los Angeles Coffee Bean Store.

★ Christina Aguilera always demands that all the catering equipment she uses on tour should be environmentally friendly. Aguilera has also been known to instruct her bouncers to clear the toilets of a London nightclub, so that she could have some privacy while using the facilities.

★ While filming *A Few Good Men*, Tom Cruise made sure his contract included a clause that guaranteed that his trailer would be closer to the set than that of any other actor in the film.

★ When giving interviews, Latin heart-throb Ricky Martin is said to request orange tinting in the lighting to highlight his golden suntan.

★ Health-conscious movie star Julia Roberts has been known to request a constant supply of organic milk in her trailer during filming.

★ Before she gets on a plane, Diana Ross is said to demand that her seat is disinfected, and that the plane toilet is stocked with her specified brand of toilet paper.

★ Justin Timberlake once demanded that a hotel he was staying in put up screens from the hotel lift to the front door, so fans could be kept away as he left the building.

FACTS ABOUT FAMOUS COMEDIANS
AND COMIC ACTORS

They make us laugh with their quick wit and gags, but what do we really know about those who have us rolling in the aisles?

★ *Never Mind the Buzzcocks* panellist Phil Jupitus used to be the Housemartins' press officer. While on tour with the band he started telling jokes on stage, which led to his career in comedy.

★ And before becoming a stand-up comedian himself, *Never Mind the Buzzcocks* presenter Mark Lamarr performed as a poet.

★ Nicholas Lyndhurst had to watch his mother's *Only Fools and Horses* video collection to remember how to do Rodney's voice when he returned to film the 1996 trilogy.

★ Julian Clary suffers from regular panic attacks, one of which occurred during Ruby Wax's chatshow.

★ Pamela Stephenson stood in the 1987 General Election as a candidate for the 'I want to drop blancmange down Terry Wogan's Y-Fronts' Party.

★ John Cleese and Connie Booth took six weeks to write each episode of *Fawlty Towers*. The norm is ten days, but the pair included every glance and gesture in the script, which meant each show was 120 pages long as opposed to 65. Cleese got the idea for the sitcom while staying at a hotel in Torquay with the Monty Python team. At one point during their stay, the eccentric proprietor of the hotel threw

Eric Idle's briefcase into the street, because he believed it was a bomb.

★ Wealthy comedian Harry Enfield used to live with Paul Whitehouse in Hackney, but never gave him a penny the whole time he was there.

★ Ruby Wax once set fire to billionaire businessman Bill Gates's eyebrow.

★ Comic actor Mike Myers wrote the script for *Wayne's World* in just three weeks. The film grossed over $200 million.

★ Myers' professional career began the day he graduated from high school. He took his final exams at nine o'clock in the morning, auditioned for Toronto's famed 'Second City' comedy troupe at noon, and was hired at three o'clock in the afternoon.

★ *Pink Panther* and *Goons* legend Peter Sellers was very superstitious. He would never wear the colour green.

★ Ken Dodd has his own 'giggle map' of Britain. It tells him what makes people laugh in different parts of the country.

★ *Cold Feet* star John Thomson had a reading age of 18 and an IQ of 186 when he was only seven years old. Thomson is also a semi-professional drummer. He has been having lessons since he was eleven.

★ Victoria Wood has claimed that she keeps her tonsils in shape by gargling with Fairy Liquid.

★ Eddie Izzard wanted to work as an accountant when he was young.

★ *Whose Line is it Anyway?* star Tony Slattery has a black belt in judo.

★ *Friends* star Matt Le Blanc may not have got into acting if it hadn't been for his mother who, fearing for his safety, encouraged him to pursue something other than professional motorcycle racing.

★ *Shooting Stars* host and Middlesbrough supporter Bob Mortimer once lost a tooth when a supporter from a rival team threw a can at him.

★ US comedian and comic actor Richard Pryor was brought up in a brothel.

★ Stephen Fry wrote the West End and Broadway musical *Me and My Girl*.

★ Long-running comedy show *The Two Ronnies* only came into being by accident. Ronnie Barker and Ronnie Corbett were presenting the BAFTAs one year when a technical hitch occurred. The pair covered the problem so well that producers offered them their own show.

★ Johnny Vegas reportedly attended interviews for theological college and was accepted by the priesthood. He changed his mind at the last minute.

★ Vegas also sold his wedding photos to *Viz* magazine for £1.

★ Frank Skinner received 131 complaints after his first television appearance in 1988. One came from the then Tory MP Edwina Currie.

★ When Frank Skinner and comedy partner David Baddiel were writing the lyrics for 'Three Lions', the England football anthem for Euro '96, they originally included the line 'Terry Butcher at war', a reference to Butcher's bravery in continuing to play a match against Sweden after sustaining a bad head injury during the game. The FA refused to allow the line, saying the phrase 'at war' could conjure up images of football hooliganism, so the line was replaced with 'Bobby belting the ball'.

★ *Phoenix Nights* star Peter Kay actually has a qualification in stand-up, which he got as part of his BTEC in Media Performance Studies. Kay's childhood ambition was to be a bin man.

★ *Goodness Gracious Me* star Meera Syal was called 'Fuzz' at school by her music teacher. This was partly to do with her big hair and also the fact that her real name is Feroza.

★ Dom Joly's middle name is Romulus, because he was conceived in Rome.

★ *Blackadder* star Rowan Atkinson is the youngest person to star in a West End one-man show. He was 26 at the time.

★ *Smack the Pony* star Doon MacKichan is a keen swimmer and has successfully swum across the English Channel.

★ MacKichan swallowed a tiddlywink when she was eight, and had to undergo a three-hour operation to have it removed.

★ Ronnie Barker secretly contributed to *The Two Ronnies* as a writer for several years, under the name Gerald Wiley. Eventually, the production team arranged a meeting with Wiley, who was said to have written almost three-quarters of all the material used. They were surprised when Barker turned up, saying that he wanted to make sure that his material was chosen for its quality, not just because of who he was.

★ While he was at university, Graham Norton used to collect dead flies.

★ Billy Connolly was once banjo player for the folk band The Humblebums. Also in the group was Gerry Rafferty, who is famous for his song 'Baker Street'.

★ Playing the banjo was Connolly's first paid job in entertainment. However, while performing he forgot the words of his song and resorted to finishing the story by simply telling it. The audience started laughing at the spoken version, and Billy's act was born.

★ Alistair McGowan's fellow impressionist Ronni Ancona discovered she had a talent for voices while working on a paddle steamer with tourists. She used to make the visitors laugh with her impressions of Hollywood film stars such as Marilyn Monroe and Shirley Temple.

★ Jimmy Tarbuck owns the number plate COM 1C.

★ Rik Mayall and Adrian Edmondson were reportedly planning to call their 90s sitcom *Your Bottom*, so viewers could say, 'I saw *Your Bottom* on television last night.' They later settled on *Bottom*.

★ While Arthur Smith was studying at the University of East Anglia, writer Malcolm Bradbury marked one of his essays. He gave him a B-minus and suggested that he stick to comedy.

★ In an attempt to persuade Jerry Seinfeld to continue making his popular show beyond its ninth series, the comedian was reportedly offered $5 million per episode by the television network that made it. Seinfeld declined.

★ David Jason's Del Boy is now regarded as one of the all-time great comedy creations. However, when *Only Fools and Horses* began, it wasn't very successful. It was only when there was a technician's strike at the BBC that the series was repeated and became a smash hit.

★ *Pink Panther* star Peter Sellers got his break in broadcasting when he duped a BBC producer, by using the voice of Kenneth Horne, a famous performer at the time. The producer was so impressed by his impressionist skills that he gave Sellers a small part in a comedy show.

★ *Shooting Stars* host Vic Reeves met comedy partner Bob

Mortimer when Bob, who was then working as a solicitor, got on stage to heckle Vic during an early performance of his *Big Night Out* show in a London pub.

★ Bob Mortimer takes a CD player with him wherever he goes in the world, because he likes to dance. He has said that if he and Vic are on location together they often dance for hours.

★ John Inman was the only member of the original British *Are You Being Served?* cast to appear in the Australian version of the sitcom. This was reportedly because they were unable to find anyone else who was camp enough for the role of Mr Humphries.

★ In his entry for *Who's Who*, John Cleese lists his hobbies as 'gluttony and sloth'.

★ As a teenager Vic Reeves played in a rock band called Trout. It didn't last long.

★ Ken Dodd is in the *Guinness Book of Records* for telling 1,500 jokes in three and a half hours.

★ Dodd has his tickling sticks made especially for him, and gets through hundreds every year.

★ Jane Leeves, who appears as Daphne in *Frasier*, was once one of Benny Hill's 'Angels'.

★ Stephen Fry claims to hold the UK record for uttering the most profanities on television during one live broadcast.

★ At 24, Jim Davidson was the youngest ever comedian to appear at the London Palladium.

★ Ruby Wax's parents were Austrian Jews, who fled Europe and Hitler in 1938 and found refuge in the United States.

★ In *Who's Who*, along with cricket, tennis and opera, Rory Bremner lists one of his hobbies as 'stress'.

★ Impressionist Alistair McGowan is allergic to wig glue.

★ Graham Norton was the victim of a serious knife attack when he was 26. He lost half the blood in his body and one of his lungs collapsed.

★ Norton initially wanted to be an actor and went to the Central School of Drama in London. He was determined to be a serious actor because he thought being funny was a cop-out.

★ Norton is the only person to have a talking waxwork at Madame Tussaud's.

★ John Cleese and his wife always buy two copies of new books to read at the same time, so they can discuss them together.

★ *Mr Bean* creator Rowan Atkinson sold his famous comic creation to 94 countries and 53 airlines.

★ Paul Merton was a shy child. He has said that he used to spend whole days in bed reading every book he could find on silent-film legends Charlie Chaplin and Buster Keaton.

FACTS ABOUT FAMOUS PRESENTERS

We always feel we know what radio and television presenters are really like because, unlike actors and actresses, we believe they are being themselves when they are on air.

But there are always some things we don't know.

★ When he was still training to be a chef, Gary Rhodes was run down by a tram and had to undergo brain surgery.

★ Rhodes initially learned to cook when he was looking after his younger sister, while his mother was at work.

★ The house that garden designer Diarmuid Gavin currently lives in with his wife in Harlesden, London, contains the first garden that Diarmuid has actually owned himself.

★ A favourite with the ladies, one of Diarmuid's fans once broke into his hotel room and tried to climb into bed with him.

★ Country music presenter 'Whispering' Bob Harris co-founded *Time Out* magazine in 1968.

★ John Peel was a DJ for WRR radio in Dallas in the 1960s. He was present when Jack Ruby shot Lee Harvey Oswald.

★ *Weakest Link* host Anne Robinson's first reporting job on a national newspaper, the *Daily Mail*, ended when she married the new deputy editor, Charles Wilson. He didn't think it strange to sack her at his editor's request because of a rule that banned married couples from working together.

★ Anne Robinson developed her trademark wink when, in

1987, the director of the BBC's right-to-reply show *Points of View* asked her *not* to wink. She subsequently winked at the end of every programme.

★ *Fifteen to One* presenter William G Stewart produced and directed the 70s sitcom *Bless This House*, which starred Sid James.

★ *Treasure Hunt* presenter Suzi Perry's uncle was a member of the rock group Whitesnake.

★ David Frost has trained as a lay preacher.

★ *The Sky at Night* presenter Patrick Moore has no formal qualifications and taught himself astronomy.

★ Patrick Moore was once broadcasting live when a fly flew towards him. As he drew breath, the fly flew into his mouth. Moore felt it was rude to spit the fly out, and could not wait for it to fly out again, so he simply swallowed it and continued broadcasting as if nothing had happened.

★ Royal correspondent Jennie Bond once received a message from Diana, Princess of Wales, telling her to wear red on television because it suited her.

★ Former *Pop Idol* hopeful-turned-presenter Hayley Evetts had eight months off school and saw her weight drop to just six and a half stone when she was fourteen, after contracting tuberculosis.

★ On entering the world of show business, Bruce Forsyth decided that he wanted to call himself Jack Johnson. Unfortunately there was already a heavyweight boxer of the same name, so he stuck with his own.

★ Phillip Schofield was ten when he wrote to all the Radio 1 presenters, asking them for advice on how to become a DJ. The only one to reply was Annie Nightingale.

★ Celebrity chef Anthony Worrall Thompson's first job after

leaving catering college was in Essex. It is rumoured that his grandmother refused to write to him because she couldn't bring herself to write the word 'Essex' on the envelope.

★ Melvyn Bragg, host of *The South Bank Show*, used to try and pull girls as a teenager by pretending that he was a famous poet. The girls fell for it, and him.

★ *This Morning*'s medical expert, Dr Chris Steele, was Richard and Judy's family GP in Manchester. They recommended him to the show's producers.

★ *Liquid News* presenter Claudia Winkleman failed her driving test five times.

★ When *Desert Island Discs* presenter Sue Lawley appeared as a guest on her own show, she chose an endless supply of Egyptian sheets as her luxury item.

★ Carol Vorderman's great-grandfather has two butterflies, several insects, and a worm named after him.

★ *GMTV* presenter Eamonn Holmes shared a bedroom with his brother until he was 26.

★ Fellow presenter Fiona Phillips can play the trombone.

★ Radio 2 presenter Don Maclean has had his tonsils removed twice – once when he was a child, and again as an adult because they had grown back.

★ ITV1 weather presenter Sian Lloyd once had to spit out chewing gum live on air. It landed on her weather map, on her native Wales.

★ Judy Finnegan got her job as a local television reporter, after giving programme bosses an eight-minute talk about Manchester United.

★ While working in local radio, Finnegan's husband Richard

Madeley used to memorise scripts and speak into a radio microphone, in preparation for his days in front of the camera.

★ *This Morning* psychiatrist Dr Raj Persaud enjoys visiting local psychiatric hospitals when he goes abroad.

★ Before joining *Changing Rooms*, Laurence Llewelyn-Bowen designed industrial flooring for Buckingham Palace, the Royal Albert Hall and London Underground.

★ In the fishing village in Cornwall where he has a house, Laurence is known as 'Darth', because of the long leather coat he wears.

★ Sir David Attenborough once thought he was suffering from malaria when he woke up covered in sweat, after several months away filming in exotic lands. He later discovered that his wife had bought an electric blanket in his absence.

★ Jamie Oliver is dyslexic.

★ Despite being one of the world's most famous Chinese cooks, Ken Hom was actually born in Tucson, Arizona. He didn't like American food, however, so his mother would send him to school with a hot flask of stir-fried vegetables and rice.

★ Sir David Attenborough got into presenting by accident. He was working behind the scenes of the programme *Zoo Quest* when the presenter became ill. He was told to take over because there was 'no one else'.

★ Cilla Black made her television comeback with *Surprise Surprise!* in 1984. The show was devised for her after television executives saw her appear on *Wogan* some months earlier and take over the show.

★ Jamie Theakston is a member of MENSA.

★ *Bargain Hunt*'s David Dickinson also came into TV by chance, after going to a barbecue at his daughter's house and meeting her neighbour, a TV executive, who said that Dickinson reminded him of Lovejoy, the fictional antiques dealer.

★ When Dickinson's wife first met him, she told him that his hair reminded her of a lion and she also thought he was gay.

★ Dermot O'Leary enjoys mackerel fishing.

★ Goodie-turned-ornithologist Bill Oddie was the fifth most successful songwriter in the country in 1975, after several surprise hits with the Goodies.

★ *Ground Force* presenter Tommy Walsh got into television after meeting the executive producer of the show while doing some building work on her house. She asked his opinion on various pilots and was so impressed by his knowledge that she invited him to screen-test with another unknown named Charlie Dimmock, and they both joined the *Ground Force* team.

★ *Changing Room's* 'Handy' Andy Kane also got into television by chance. He was doing some carpentry work for fellow presenter Linda Barker when she invited him to come and work on the show. He thought she wanted him to build the scenery, so he agreed.

★ When Nelson Mandela met Charlie Dimmock, he told her she looked like a Spice Girl.

★ Eamonn Andrews was the first guest on *This Is Your Life*.

★ Rick Stein did not always plan to cook for a living. He only trained as a chef after his attempts at running a nightclub proved unsuccessful.

★ Noel Edmonds got his big break in radio standing in for Kenny Everett when he was off sick.

★ Anna Ford was thirty when she joined Granada television as a researcher in 1974. She was told at the time that she was too old to be a newsreader – four years later she was presenting the news on ITN.

★ *Grandstand* presenter Ray Stubbs only moved into broadcasting after an earlier career on the sporting field. He joined Tranmere Rovers from school and was on the club's books for five years before moving to an administrative role with the club.

★ Ulrika Jonsson wears a mouth-guard while she sleeps, to stop her grinding her teeth.

★ When she was young, Ulrika was asked to appear in a remake of *Peter Pan* by Hollywood director Steven Spielberg. Her mum said no.

★ Trendy *T4* presenter June Sarpong has never drunk alcohol or smoked.

★ Chris Tarrant lived in a van for six months while working as a supply teacher at a school in London. He parked the van just outside the school gates.

★ *The City Gardener*, Matt James, doesn't have a garden of his own – he only has a balcony.

★ Jeremy Beadle was once voted the second-most hated man by the British, just behind Saddam Hussein.

★ Before becoming one of the designers on BBC's *Changing Rooms*, Linda Barker did private work for both Cilla Black and hypnotist Paul McKenna.

★ American talk-show host Jerry Springer was actually born in London. His parents were German Jews who had escaped to England before the Holocaust began.

★ Bob Monkhouse is one of the leading collectors and historians of the work of Laurel and Hardy.

★ Gary Lineker was so disturbed by impressionist Alistair

McGowan's mimicry of his facial movements that he has tried to change his behaviour on *Match of the Day*.

★ Lineker's middle name is Winston because he was born on Winston Churchill's birthday – 30 November.

★ As a fifteen-year-old pop wannabe with the group Faith, Hope and Charity, Dani Behr pretended to be dating George Michael in order to help promote the group's first single.

★ Behr is nicknamed 'Mountie' – because she always gets her man.

★ Magician Paul Daniels has the registration number MAG 1C on his Bentley.

★ He may have spent several weeks in the jungle, but *I'm a Celebrity ... Get Me Out of Here* presenter Ant McPartlin is terrified of spiders.

★ Meanwhile, Ant's partner in crime, Declan Donnelly, has his own phobia – he is scared of pigeons.

★ When chef Clarissa Dickson-Wright won a place at Oxford University to study law, her father refused to subsidise her unless she changed her degree to medicine. She refused to change courses and was called to the bar at the age of 21.

★ Oprah Winfrey was actually named Orpah, a name taken from the Book of Ruth in the Bible. It was mis-spelt on her birth certificate.

★ Dale Winton's mother, Sheree, appeared in the Beatles' film *A Hard Day's Night*, and also had a walk-on part in the James Bond film *Thunderball*.

★ Born in Belfast, *Fame Academy* presenter Patrick Kielty is the son of a builder who was shot dead by the Ulster Freedom Fighters.

★ Delia Smith gave up cookery writing in the 1980s to concentrate on writing religious books. During the whole of the decade she only brought out one cookery book, and that was a reissue.

★ Carol Vorderman got her television break on *Countdown* after her mum spotted an advert in a local newspaper for a television presenter who was good at maths. She applied for the job on Carol's behalf.

★ Cat Deeley was signed up by Storm modelling agency at the age of fourteen but refused to commit to modelling until after her education.

★ Rolf Harris played didgeridoo on Kate Bush's 'The Dreaming'.

★ *Top Gear* presenter Jeremy Clarkson was a big fan of Princess Diana and says he bought a flat opposite her gym to catch glimpses of her.

★ When Delia Smith declared that her omelette pan was 'a little gem' during the first series of *How to Cook*, annual sales of the pan rose from 200 to 140,000, with 90,000 being sold in the first four months. The small company that manufactured the pans went from facing bankruptcy to having to recruit extra staff to cope with the massive increase in demand.

★ Former *RI:SE* presenter Mark Durden-Smith spent a month in a New Zealand hospital with second-degree burns, after falling into a geyser. Someone was taking a photograph of him, when he fell in.

★ Sir David Frost didn't learn to swim until he was an adult.

★ Anthony Worrall Thompson swam the English Channel when he was sixteen.

★ Trinidadian-born newsreader Sir Trevor McDonald learned 'to speak properly' by copying announcers on the BBC's World Service.

★ Barry Norman had many political arguments with actor John Wayne, which ended up one day with Wayne getting up and attempting to thump him.

★ Talk-show host Trisha Goddard once spent five weeks in a psychiatric hospital. She is now a trained counsellor and a mental health campaigner.

★ Goddard was the first black primetime anchorperson on Australian TV.

★ *Gardener's World* presenter Rachel de Thame was once a professional ballet dancer.

★ As the Queen presented *Ground Force's* Alan Titchmarsh with his MBE for services to horticulture and broadcasting, she told him, 'You've given a lot of ladies a lot of pleasure.'

★ Before becoming a broadcaster, Jimmy Young was a successful pop star. He got to number one in the 1950s with his version of 'Unchained Melody'. When he originally recorded the track he was suffering from severe stomach pain. The recording session took place just after one o'clock at a studio in Hampstead, and less than one hour later Young was undergoing an emergency operation at the University College Hospital in London.

★ Delia Smith didn't start cooking seriously until she was in her twenties. Her boyfriend prompted the move at the time, as he kept singing the praises of his former girlfriend's culinary skills.

★ Esther Rantzen was to have been a member of the original TV-AM line-up when the station launched in 1983, but pulled out when she discovered she was pregnant.

★ Madame Tussaud's regularly has to clean the lipstick off Alan Titchmarsh's waxwork.

★ Many years before he joined *Monty Python's Flying Circus* and long before he set off *Around the World in Eighty Days*, Michael Palin planned to be an explorer.

★ Angela Rippon had dreams of being a ballet dancer when she was a child, but grew too tall. Her mother originally took her to classes when she was three, because she was knock-kneed.

★ While working in regional television, Richard Madeley was nicknamed 'The Mannequin', because of his immaculate appearance.

★ Chat-show king Michael Parkinson had two ambitions as a boy. One was not to follow his father down the mines, the other was to play cricket for his beloved Yorkshire. He didn't achieve either, but didn't do too badly after all.

★ Channel 5 newsreader Kirsty Young has never had any formal journalistic training.

★ Chris Evans was once sacked from the newsagents he was working in, for cranking up the volume of the shop's radio too loudly.

★ Presenter of *The Club*, Donna Air, was nicknamed Lego Legs when she was a child.

★ Clarissa Dickson-Wright is one of only two women in England to ever become a guild butcher. The other was the Queen Mother.

★ *Channel 4 News* presenter Jon Snow turned down an OBE in 2000.

★ *GMTV* presenter Eamonn Holmes cannot swim.

★ Jerry Springer worked on Robert Kennedy's aborted presidential election campaign.

★ Rolf Harris had a stand-up row with John Lennon in 1963,

after Lennon heckled Harris while he was performing in a show.

★ While presenting *The Rolf Harris Show*, Harris used to rehearse his huge landscape paintings as many as five times before he recorded each programme. He would always paint them full size and against the clock, to ensure that he could complete them in the allotted time.

★ Bruce Forsyth was evacuated to Clacton when the Second World War broke out, but he returned home to London after only three days, because he was so homesick.

★ Graham Norton was so nervous at the prospect of presenting his own show, *So Graham Norton*, that in the weeks leading up to the start of the first series he suffered from insomnia and panic attacks.

FACTS ABOUT FAMOUS ACTORS
AND ACTRESSES

If we are honest, most of us at some stage have dreamed about being an actor and starring in a Hollywood blockbuster – even if it's just so we could kiss Brad Pitt and George Clooney, or perhaps grab a feel of Jennifer Lopez's much talked about bottom.

Their lives seem to be one long round of glamorous premiers and award ceremonies, designer dresses and glittering jewels, but what goes on behind all the cosmetic dentistry and beautifully manicured nails?

★ Halle Berry reportedly refused to bathe for weeks in preparation for her role as a crack addict in Spike Lee's *Jungle Fever*.

★ When Tamzin Outhwaite attended the London Studio Centre, she won the cup for the most outstanding all-rounder. Her name was engraved immediately below the previous year's winner of the award – Liz Hurley.

★ The father of *Friends* star Matthew Perry, actor John Bennett Perry, appeared in Old Spice commercials in the 70s.

★ *Deer Hunter* star Christopher Walken began his career as a dancer.

★ *The Usual Suspects* star Gabriel Byrne didn't start acting until he was 29, and he only went to America for the first time when he was 37.

★ Bond Girl Honor Blackman was offered the choice of a bike

or elocution lessons for her fifteenth birthday. She thought her cockney accent was too strong, so decided to enrol in the Guildhall School of Music and Drama.

★ Actress Winona Ryder was named after the town where her family lived in Minnesota.

★ Before moving into acting, *Friends* star Lisa Kudrow studied biology, and was part of a medical study that made break-throughs in the understanding of headaches.

★ Woody Allen claims that he has never watched any of his work.

★ Pamela Anderson, Sharon Stone, Jane Seymour, Madonna, Elle MacPherson and Kim Basinger have all bared all for *Playboy* magazine.

★ Kiefer Sutherland's full name is Kiefer William Frederick Dempsey George Rufus Sutherland.

★ Sylvester Stallone grew up in a foster home until he was five years old.

★ When actor Robin Williams auditioned for the role of Mork in *Mork and Mindy*, he met the producer, who told him to sit down. Robin immediately sat on his head on the chair. The producer immediately chose him, saying that he was the only alien who auditioned.

★ And during the making of *Mork and Mindy* Williams departed from the scripts and ad-libbed so many times, and so well, that the producers stopped trying to make him stick to the script. In fact they began to deliberately leave gaps in the later scripts – noting only 'Mork can go off here' –so Robin could improvise.

★ Tom Baker may never have become *Dr Who* if it hadn't been for the sitcom *Porridge*. Fulton MacKay was regarded as the favourite to take over from Jon Pertwee, but he chose to play prison officer Mr Mackay opposite Ronnie Barker instead.

★ Niamh Cusack, who starred as Dr Kate Rowan in *Heartbeat* and Christine Fletcher in hospital drama *A&E*, can't stand the sight of blood. When researching her role for *A&E*, she passed out after a boy came in with his finger sawn off.

★ *Ripley's Game* star John Malkovich is a director as well as an actor, and was due to direct a version of *The Talented Mr Ripley* during the 1980s. In the end, the film was not made.

★ Known for his dedication to his roles, Daniel Day-Lewis trained for two and a half years for his role in *The Boxer*, and sparred over five hundred rounds. He also remained in a wheelchair in between takes while filming *My Left Foot*, and became ill during the filming of *Gangs of New York* because he refused to wear anything more than his character's threadbare coat while shooting during the cold winter months.

★ Tom Hanks did not always harbour ambitions to appear in front of a camera. After leaving school he studied stage carpentry at college, and was so talented his skills won him a scholarship to California State University.

★ Martial arts star Bruce Lee was meant to be so fast that producers sometimes slowed the film down so that you could see his moves.

★ After leaving drama school, *Inspector Morse* star Kevin Whately spent time as a folk singer.

★ *Absolutely Fabulous* star Joanna Lumley came up with the idea for the sitcom *Are You Being Served?* At the time, she was married to the show's creator Jeremy Lloyd.

★ After Clark Gable appeared in the film *It Happened One Night*, without wearing a vest, sales of undershirts throughout America dropped dramatically.

★ Al Pacino is reported to have originally asked for $7 million to appear in the 1990 film *The Godfather: Part III*. His excessive demands annoyed director Francis Ford Coppola so much that he threatened to write a new script that opened with Michael Corleone's funeral! Pacino settled for $5 million.

★ Kim Basinger nicknamed Mickey Rourke 'The Human Ashtray', after working with him on the film *9 1/2 Weeks*.

★ *I Love Lucy* star Desi Arnaz and movie legend Orson Welles both owned the film rights to the book *Dead Calm*, after it was published in the 1960s. It took over twenty years for the film to be made with Nicole Kidman and Billy Zane in the lead roles.

★ Melanie Griffith's mother is actress Tippi Hedren, best known for her lead role in Alfred Hitchcock's *The Birds*. When Griffith was six years old, she received a birthday present from Hitchcock. On opening it, she found that the gift was not a doll as expected, but a miniature version of her mother in a tiny coffin.

★ When Frances McDormand won the Best Actress Oscar in 1996 for her role in *Fargo*, she became the first star to win in a film directed by a spouse – husband Joel Coen.

★ Actress Amanda Holden was in the original line-up for the comedy series *Smack the Pony*. When she left she was replaced by Doon MacKichan.

★ Richard Gere was once banned from the Oscars for making anti-China statements on the air.

★ Judi Dench originally spelled her Christian name with a 'y'. She changed it when she arrived at the Central School of Drama and found there was another girl called Judy in her class.

★ Kevin Costner was working in marketing when a chance meeting with film legend Richard Burton changed his life.

Burton told him to commit to acting fully if that was what he wanted to do. Costner immediately resigned from his job and moved to Hollywood.

★ *Clocking Off* and *Where the Heart Is* star Pam Ferris was 34 when she made her first appearance on television.

★ For a long time Carmen Electra never had her own name on a bathing suit, when she was appearing in *Baywatch*. She was always given one that said Pamela (Anderson) or Yasmine (Bleeth). When she eventually earned her own suit, at the end of the season's filming, she had it framed.

★ Michael Douglas got his big break when he persuaded his father, Kirk Douglas, to sell him the rights to the film *One Flew over the Cuckoo's Nest*.

★ John Malkovich was a plump child, and only lost weight after going on a crash diet of jelly for several months.

★ Barbara Windsor only appeared in nine of the thirty *Carry On* films.

★ Former *EastEnder* Martin Kemp once featured in the *Roy of the Rovers* comics. He appeared as a player for Melchester Rovers during the 1985–86 season.

★ Mary Crosby, the daughter of film legend Bing, played Kristin Shepherd, the *Dallas* character that shot JR in 1980.

★ After being dropped from a film contract in the 1970s, one studio executive told Harrison Ford, 'You ain't got it, kid.' Ford went on to become one of the biggest film stars in Hollywood.

★ Actress Britt Ekland can be heard puffing and panting at the end of the Rod Stewart record 'Tonight's the Night'.

★ Leonardo DiCaprio got his name after he kicked his mother, while still in the womb, while she was looking at some Leonardo di Vinci paintings.

★ Cher has played herself in two films – *Good Times* and *The Player*.

★ According to Paul Hogan, when he decided to make *Crocodile Dundee*, so many people were keen to invest in the film that he had to send back $3.5 million.

★ Angelina Jolie had a crush on *Star Trek's* Mr Spock when she was a child.

★ Clive Hornby, who plays Jack Sugden in *Emmerdale*, was the drummer for a 60s Liverpool band called The Dennisons. They were billed as 'the next big thing' and looked set to follow the Beatles. Unfortunately worldwide fame was not around the corner.

★ Cynthia Nixon, who plays Miranda in *Sex and the City*, doesn't really have red hair. She has to dye it every few weeks.

★ Sigourney Weaver has a fear of lifts.

★ *Lord of the Rings* and *Star Wars* star Christopher Lee speaks seven languages.

★ *Auf Wiedersehen, Pet* star Timothy Spall was mistaken for a window cleaner on his first day at RADA.

★ Matt Damon lost forty pounds for his role as a Gulf War veteran in the film *Courage Under Fire*.

★ Keanu Reeves bathed in a pool of ice in preparation for his part in *Matrix Reloaded*. Reeves also underwent kung fu training for at least seven hours a day in order to be convincing as the central character of Neo.

★ Clint Eastwood owned the script for the film *Unforgiven* for many years, but didn't make the movie until he felt he was old enough to play the lead character.

★ Ben Affleck's middle name is Geza.

★ *My Family* actress Zoë Wanamaker was born in New York,

but grew up in England after her father Sam was blacklisted during the McCarthy witch-hunts.

★ Donald Sutherland began his career in show business at the age of fourteen, as a radio DJ.

★ Universal studios sacked Burt Reynolds in the 1960s, because 'he couldn't act'. Ten years later the same studios re-signed him for £1 million.

★ *Heartbeat's* Greengrass, actor Bill Maynard, once stood against Tony Benn as an independent candidate in a Chesterfield by-election.

★ George Clooney owns a pet pig called Max, which was given to him by actress Kelly Preston (who is now married to John Travolta) when she was going out with him.

★ Gary Oldman had to be treated for malnutrition after starving himself in preparation for his part as Sid Vicious in the 1986 film *Sid and Nancy*.

★ Ewan McGregor is an accomplished French horn player.

★ Star of *The Hours*, Julianne Moore, was told not to be too hopeful about building a successful career as an actress, as redheads were hard to cast.

★ *EastEnders* actress Jill Halfpenny, who plays undercover police officer Kate Tyler, once dated her *Byker Grove* co-star Ant McPartlin.

★ Barbara Windsor was considering becoming a showbiz agent, when she was cast in the role of Peggy Mitchell in *EastEnders*.

★ When Sid James wasn't available to star in the 1967 film *Carry On ... Follow that Camel*, the film's producers wanted Woody Allen to play his part. They thought an American would widen the appeal of the film to the US market, and thought Allen would be suitable as he had recently risen to fame in the film *What's New Pussycat?* He declined and the part went to Phil Silvers.

★ *Hornblower* star Ioan Gruffudd had to give up playing his favourite sport of rugby when he became an actor, because the risk of injury was considered to be too high.

★ Sir Laurence Olivier may be regarded as one of Britain's greatest actors of all time, but he was not so talented in the air. When World War II began he qualified as a pilot in the Fleet Air Arm. However, on the discovery that Olivier was so incompetent that he had destroyed five aircraft in only seven weeks, he was seconded into propaganda entertainment by the Ministry of Information and didn't see any active service.

★ When Kylie Minogue first joined the cast of *Neighbours* as tomboy Charlene, she earned only £150 per week. By the time she left the soap two years later, her wages had risen to over £1000 per week.

★ *Moonlighting* star Cybill Shepherd was named Cybill by combining the names of her grandfather (Cy) and her father (Bill).

★ Laila Morse, who plays Mo Harris in *EastEnders*, got her acting break in the film *Nil by Mouth*, which was directed by her actor brother, Gary Oldman.

★ Kelsey Grammer sings and plays the piano on the theme song of *Frasier*.

★ Jessie Wallace, *EastEnders*' Kat Slater, was suspended from the show for two months without pay in 2003, in punishment for bad behaviour off screen.

★ Even though everyone refers to him as an Italian-American actor, Robert de Niro is mainly Irish in ancestry.

★ *Dalziel and Pascoe* star Colin Buchanan is actually a Scot – he was born in Dundee – but he hides his accent in the series.

★ Samuel L Jackson originally auditioned for a musical while studying architecture at university, because his speech therapist thought it might help his stutter.

★ *Legally Blonde* actress Reese Witherspoon uses the third of her Christian names. The first two are Laura Jean.

★ Western legend John Wayne studied dance so he would walk better on screen.

★ Many years before he played Father Peter in *Ballykissangel*, Stephen Tompkinson considered a career as a priest.

★ Jim Carrey's make-up for *The Mask* took four hours each day to apply.

★ When Harrison Ford got his star on the Hollywood Walk of Fame in 2003, it was not the first time his name had appeared on the famous sidewalk. A less well-known 60s film star, also called Harrison Ford, already had one on there.

★ Ripley, the character brought to life by Sigourney Weaver in *Alien*, was originally written as a man.

★ While pregnant with her daughter Carys, Catherine Zeta Jones developed a craving for Marmite, and would often send her husband Michael Douglas on long journeys to find some.

★ *Blues Brothers* star Dan Aykroyd was once engaged to Carrie Fisher.

★ Renee Zellweger put on twenty pounds for her role in *Bridget Jones's Diary*.

★ Marilyn Monroe was rumoured to sew buttons inside her clothes to make it appear as if her nipples were sticking out.

★ *EastEnders* star Shane Richie has a tattoo saying 'Co' on his bottom, which he decided to get when he was drunk with Billy Idol in Los Angeles. It was supposed to be the name of his wife at the time, former Nolan sister Coleen, but he stopped the tattooist halfway through because the pain was too much to bear.

★ Keanu Reeves was born in the Lebanon.

★ Jamie Lee Curtis also goes under the name Lady Haden-Guest – her husband Christopher Guest has been knighted.

★ John Malkovich was nicknamed 'mad dog' by his siblings when he was a child.

★ Arthur Lowe, known to millions as Captain Mainwaring, would never allow a *Dad's Army* script in his house.

★ Charlie Sheen complained vocally when *Sopranos* star James Gandolfini pipped his dad Martin Sheen to an Emmy award. Gandolfini reportedly responded by sending Sheen Junior some rotten meat in the post.

★ Wesley Snipes got his big break when he appeared in the video for the Michael Jackson hit 'Bad'.

★ Martine McCutcheon went on two dates with Michael Douglas before he met Catherine Zeta Jones.

★ *Friends* star Courtney Cox appeared as Bruce Springsteen's dance partner in his video for 'Dancing in the Dark'.

★ The parents of action star Jackie Chan almost sold him to the doctor who delivered him because they couldn't pay his medical bills.

★ Until he was eighteen, Woody Allen read almost nothing except comic books. He did show his writing skills, however, by selling one-liners for 10 cents each to gossip columnists.

★ *At Home with the Braithwaites* star Amanda Redman is a qualified drama teacher and still runs a weekend theatre school.

★ Oscar winner Denzel Washington got into acting after a summer holiday spent as a YMCA camp counsellor. To entertain the campers, he took part in a counsellor talent show. He received such praise from the audience that he took up drama lessons.

★ Fred Astaire was not a trained dancer.

★ Marilyn Monroe appeared nude in the first edition of *Playboy*, published in 1953.

★ Roger Moore, Michael Caine, Clint Eastwood and Sophia Loren all started their careers as film extras.

★ *Four Weddings and a Funeral* actor Simon Callow wrote a letter to Sir Laurence Olivier when he was eighteen. Callow says the letter contained such enthusiasm for his National Theatre at the Old Vic that Olivier replied by return of post offering Callow a job in the box office.

★ In the late 80s Patrick Swayze signed for a film called *Total Recall*. Unfortunately the movie fell through, but reappeared several years later with Arnold Schwarzengger in the lead role.

★ Actresses Leslie Ash and Michelle Collins were both backing singers in their early career – Leslie sang with the group Smiley & Co, while Michelle sang with the beehive hair-wearing singer Mari Wilson.

★ Oscar winner Nicole Kidman is scared of butterflies.

★ Barbara Windsor was evacuated to Blackpool during the war.

★ Adam Woodyatt (Ian Beale) and Wendy Richard (Pauline Fowler) are the only members of the *EastEnders* cast to have been in the show without a break since it began in 1985.

★ *Romancing the Stone* star Kathleen Turner provided the sexy voice of Jessica Rabbit in *Who Framed Roger Rabbit?*

★ Turner's *Romancing the Stone* co-star Danny DeVito originally attended the New York American Academy of Dramatic Arts to pick up make-up tips. He had been working as a 'cosmetician' in his sister's beauty parlour, and decided to improve his skills. It was only later that he became interested in acting.

★ *Casualty* star Derek Thompson, who plays Charlie Fairhead, named his real-life son Charlie.

★ When Ben Affleck was a child, he asked his mother if he could have a dog. She tested him by making him walk an imaginary dog for a week. Ben only lasted for five days, and didn't get the dog.

★ Ronnie Barker originally wanted Paul Henry, better known as *Crossroads'* Benny, to play the part of cellmate Lenny Godber in *Porridge*. The part eventually went to Richard Beckinsale, father of actress Kate Beckinsale.

★ Hilary Swank, who won an Oscar for her performance as a cross-dresser in *Boys Don't Cry*, had swapped genders for her profession before. Her first stage role was as jungle boy Mowgli, when she was nine years old.

★ Burt Ward, who appeared as Robin in the 1960s series of *Batman*, now runs a Great Dane adoption and rescue centre in California.

★ *The Vice* star Ken Stott once fronted a band called Keyhole, before moving into acting.

★ Billy Bob Thornton has a phobia about flying and has cancelled television appearances that required him to get on a plane.

★ While his *EastEnders* character may not be very eloquent, in real life actor John Bardon, who plays Jim Branning, is an accomplished after-dinner speaker.

★ Robert Downey Jnr made his screen debut when he was just five years old, in the 1970 film *Pound*. His father, Robert Downey Snr, directed the film. The movie was about stray dogs, all played by humans. Downey Jnr played a puppy, and his first words were 'Got any hair on your balls?'

★ Downey Jnr smoked his first joint when he was eight.

★ *Green Card* star Gerard Depardieu left home when he was eight years old and lived with prostitutes until he was fifteen.

★ *Bad Girls* and *Emmerdale* star Claire King used to be in a punk band and was known to drink whisky with Lemmy from Motorhead.

★ Bing Crosby died while on a golf course.

★ *Friends'* star Courtney Cox has the phrase 'A Deal is a Deal' inscribed in her wedding ring.

★ *Peak Practice* star Kevin Whately wanted to be a doctor when he was young but thought it took too long to qualify, so he trained as an accountant instead.

★ As well as providing the voice for one of the Tellytubbies, actress and singer Toyah Wilcox was also the voice of children's favourite *Brum*.

★ Robson Green sent a fax to Francesca Annis when he heard they were to perform sex scenes together in the drama *Reckless*, saying, 'Please be careful with me.'

★ Former Monkee Mickey Dolenz auditioned for the role of 'The Fonz' in *Happy Days*.

★ When Mel Gibson flies his family to Australia he books the *whole* of the first-class section of the plane.

★ Gibson's middle name is Columcille, which means 'dove of the church'.

★ *Bull Durham* star Tim Robbins was banned from a gala screening of the movie, after he spoke out against the 2003 Iraq War.

★ Clint Eastwood got into acting after working as a delivery boy, dropping off goods and parcels at Universal studios. An employee at the studios arranged a screen test for Eastwood, who was offered $75 per week for an eighteen-month contract, during which time he had several small film roles.

★ *Coronation Street* actress Sally Lindsay was once a member of the St Winnifred's School Choir. She sung on their number one hit 'There's No-one Quite Like Grandma'.

★ *Dad's Army* star John Le Mesurier, who played Sergeant Wilson, initially thought the show would not last long as it lacked romance.

★ Although he was first to be cast for the show, David Soul originally wanted to play 'Starsky' not 'Hutch' in the 1970s series.

★ From the age of five, George Clooney spent time around his television newscaster dad's programme set. He was known to often join in while the programme was on air, shouting out the temperatures during the weather report.

★ Wendy Richard has a large collection of toy frogs.

★ Johnny Depp is terrified of clowns.

★ An agent discovered *Star Wars* actress Natalie Portman while in a pizza parlour, at the age of eleven.

★ Deena Payne, who plays Viv in *Emmerdale*, used to be a backing singer for 80s singer John Farnham.

★ When film roles dried up a few years ago, 24 star Kiefer Sutherland turned his back on Hollywood and competed in rodeos across America. He spent several months learning to rope cattle with his stunt co-ordinator from his film *The Cowboy Way*, before joining the competition circuit, and even winning several tournaments.

★ *EastEnders* hard man Phil Mitchell, aka Steve McFadden, was once hired to beat up Phil Collins in the film *Buster*.

★ James Dean only starred in three films before he was killed in a car crash. They were *East of Eden*, *Rebel Without a Cause*, and *Giant*, which was completed just three days before he died.

★ Frank Sinatra was obsessively clean, and used to shower at least four times a day.

★ As a child actress, Betty Driver, who plays *Coronation Street's* Betty Turpin, appeared in the George Formby film *Boots Boots*, in which she had a few lines of dialogue and a big song-and-dance number with Formby. Unfortunately her scenes ended up being cut from the film on the orders of Formby's domineering wife Bessie, who also appeared in the film and didn't want to be upstaged by a child.

★ *Holby City's* Alex Adams, otherwise known as Jeremy Sheffield, was a member of the Royal Ballet Company until a serious injury ended his career.

★ Sheffield has a tattoo of intertwined koi carp on his calf. He is a big fan of tropical fish and has kept them since he was a child.

★ When Kevin Bacon was twelve years old, he played in a band called 'Footloose'. Twelve years later the film of the same name made him an international star.

★ *Lord of the Ring's* star Elijah Wood appeared in the Cranberries video for the song 'Ridiculous Thought' in 1995.

★ Wood has a tattoo near his hip, which he got with some of his fellow *Lord of the Rings* cast members, including Sir Ian McKellen. It is the 'elvish' symbol of nine, to remember the real-life fellowship.

★ Amanda Holden likes to crochet.

★ James Macpherson, who played Jardine in *Taggart*, once had an interview to become a policeman but thought he was not hard enough for the job.

★ *Crocodile Dundee* star Paul Hogan made his television debut on the Australian version of *New Faces*, where he performed as a blindfolded, tap-dancing knife thrower.

★ *Speed* star Dennis Hopper has admitted that, at the peak of his hell-raising days in the 1970s, he was drinking half a gallon of rum and 28 beers every day, as well as doing three grammes of cocaine, which helped him sober up so he could start drinking again.

★ *Grease* star Olivia Newton-John represented Britain in the 1974 Eurovision song contest. She lost out to Abba.

★ After Marilyn Monroe's death in 1962, it was rumoured that she had been buried wearing a million-dollar necklace. Grave robbers attempted to get into the coffin, but were unable to break through the five hundred pounds of concrete that surrounded it.

★ Jim Carrey was always convinced he was going to make it big, and early in his career wrote himself a cheque for $20 million, which he kept in his wallet until he earned that amount for *The Cable Guy*.

★ Judi Dench once hung a notice in a theatre foyer which read: 'Miss Judi Dench does not have a cold, her voice is always like that', in a response to theatre critics who passed comment about her distinctive voice.

★ *Gladiator* star Russell Crowe's middle name is Ira.

★ Movie legend Humphrey Bogart was a familiar face to Americans when he was only a year old. His mother Maud was a commercial artist whose sketch of a little smiling Humphrey was used by a baby-food manufacturer on the labels on their product.

★ Jamie Farr, who played Klinger in *M*A*S*H*, was the only

member of the cast who actually served as a soldier in the Korean War.

★ Pauline Quirke suffers from stage fright and is said to have been sick before the filming of all episodes of *Birds of a Feather*.

★ Actress Daryl Hannah created a board game in America called 'Love It or Hate It'.

★ Although Russell Crowe's surname is of Irish extraction, he lists his background as Norwegian and Maori.

★ Martial arts star Jackie Chan weighed an enormous twelve pounds at birth.

★ Adolf Hitler was such a fan of *Gone with the Wind* legend Clark Gable that, during the Second World War, he offered a ransom to anyone who brought Gable back to him alive.

★ Tom Cruise only took an interest in acting after a knee injury ended his hopes of a career in athletics.

★ *Game On* and *Strange* star Samantha Janus represented Britain in the 1991 Eurovision Song Contest. Her song, 'A Message to You', failed to impress the judges, but it did spend three weeks in the chart.

★ *Prime Suspect* star Helen Mirren is descended from White Russian nobility.

★ Fred Astaire, Richard Burton, Peter Sellers, Marilyn Monroe, Gene Kelly, Buster Keaton, Cary Grant and Bob Hope all failed to win an Oscar during their film careers.

★ Sir Ian McKellen appeared in the video for 'Heart' by the Pet Shop Boys. He played a vampire.

★ Honor Blackman left *The Avengers* in order to take on the role of Pussy Galore in the Bond film *Goldfinger*. In her final appearance as Cathy Gale in the action series she told Patrick

MacNee's Steed, 'I'm not going to be pussyfooting along these shores.' MacNee replied, 'No pussyfooting? I must have been misinformed.'

★ Matt Damon spent part of his childhood in a commune in Boston with his mother.

★ Jennifer Lopez was the first person ever to have a hit album and hit movie at the top of the American charts on the same week.

★ Perry Fenwick won the best newcomer award at the National TV awards in 2000 for his role of Billy Mitchell in *EastEnders*, despite playing Malcolm's workmate Terry in the ITV sitcom *Watching* since 1987.

★ Elizabeth Taylor supplied the voice of baby Maggie in *The Simpsons* when she uttered her first word. She beat Whoopi Goldberg to the part.

★ Samuel L Jackson got the part of Jedi Knight Mace Windu in *Star Wars: Episode 1* after announcing on the Channel 4 programme *TFI Friday* that if there was one film he could star in, that would be the one he would choose.

★ Debra Winger was the voice of *E.T.*

★ *Friends* star Matt Le Blanc is an accomplished landscape photographer.

★ *Spiderman* actor Tobey Maguire only got into acting because of a hundred-dollar bribe from his mother. He was planning to take after his dad and train as a chef, but his mother made a deal to give him one hundred dollars if he took drama class instead.

★ Shane Richie once pulled a man from a blazing vehicle at a petrol station.

★ Hugh Grant's middle name is Mungo.

★ Legendary actor Bob Hope left school when he was nine.

★ Sigourney Weaver's father Pat was president of the American television network NBC. He is often credited as being 'The Father of the Television Talk Show'.

★ *EastEnders*' Dennis Rickman, actor Nigel Harman, is a skilled juggler.

★ *Grease* star Olivia Newton-John's career began when she won a local competition in 1960 to find a 'girl who looked most like Hayley Mills'.

★ Hollywood star Barbra Streisand suffers from tinnitus.

★ Irish heart-throb Colin Farrell made his stage debut in an Irish folk-dancing group.

★ Christopher Cazenove only decided to become an actor after the Navy rejected him as not being officer material.

★ Buddy Ebsen had to drop out from playing the role of the Tin Man in *The Wizard of Oz* in 1939, because the metallic paint made him ill.

★ Michelle Pfeiffer trained to be a court reporter.

★ Despite both receiving the same $1 million fee and percentage of box-office takings from *The Towering Inferno*, Steve McQueen was angry that fellow star Paul Newman was getting top billing over him. To solve the problem, producers decided that McQueen's name would come first in the credits and be placed to the left of Newman's in the printed posters for the film, however Newman's name would be placed slightly higher than McQueen's.

★ Gene Hackman lied about his age so he could join the Marines at sixteen.

★ *The Vice* star Ken Stott learned to play the bagpipes at

eighteen, but says he hasn't worn a kilt since he attended Sunday school.

★ Joseph Fiennes middle name is Alberic.

★ Kermit the Frog came into being in 1959. He was made out of Muppet creator Jim Henson's mum's overcoat.

★ Halle Berry is named after the Halle Building in Cleveland, Ohio, which originally housed the Halle Brothers department store. The building is now used for offices and is the fictional setting for the Winfred-Louder department store which features on US sitcom *The Drew Carey Show*.

★ In the mid-1970s former *Dynasty* actress Joan Collins had so little work, she had to claim unemployment benefit. She was recognised while queuing with other jobless people.

★ John W Hinckley was trying to impress actress Jodie Foster when he shot US President Ronald Reagan.

★ *Gladiator* star Russell Crowe played Dr Frank N Furter in the Australia and New Zealand theatre production of *The Rocky Horror Picture Show*.

★ *Lord of the Rings* star Viggo Mortensen cracked his tooth when he was hit by a sword, as well as breaking two toes, during the filming of *The Two Towers*.

★ Will Smith's nickname as a child was 'The Prince' because of his ability to charm his way out of trouble.

★ Brad Pitt chipped one of his teeth during the filming of *Fight Club*, but did not have the tooth capped until after the film was completed because he felt it added to his character.

★ 'Here's Johnny,' one of the most famous lines in *The Shining*, was improvised by Jack Nicholson.

★ Aged thirteen, Drew Barrymore was barred from pestering

fellow actor Bruce Willis.

★ Robert de Niro was so quiet when he was young that people thought he might be autistic.

★ Barbra Streisand was the first woman ever to produce, direct, write and star in a major film with her 1983 production *Yentl*.

★ Andie MacDowell's voice in *Greystoke: The Legend of Tarzan, Lord of the Apes* was dubbed by Glenn Close.

★ Stephen Fry sent author PG Wodehouse a fan letter when he was fifteen. In return he received an autographed photograph of Wodehouse. Many years later, during the filming of the Wodehouse series *Jeeves and Wooster* in which Fry starred, the photograph could be seen by eagle-eyed viewers sitting proudly on Fry's desk.

★ Emilio Estevez became the youngest Hollywood star to write, direct and star in a movie when *Wisdom* was released in 1986. He was just 23 at the time.

★ Keanu Reeves, Richard Gere, Uma Thurman, Lulu and Billy Connolly are all practising Buddhists.

★ Two days after his divorce from fellow actor Demi Moore was finalised, Bruce Willis hired forty strippers to a celebratory party at his house with a few of his friends.

★ In 1993, Hollywood star Kim Basinger was forced to pay Main Line Pictures $8.9 million, after pulling out of the movie *Boxing Helena* just one month before filming began.

★ Despite his upper-class voice, debonair actor Leslie Phillips was born the son of a Tottenham shopkeeper.

★ *Sabrina the Teenage Witch* star Melissa Joan Hart can recite the mathematical expression pi to four hundred decimal places.

★ John Le Mesurier, who played Sergeant Wilson in *Dad's Army*, was the voice of children's character Bod.

★ Martine McCutcheon got a place at the Italia Conti stage school after writing to two hundred companies and charities asking them to help her with her fees. *EastEnders* was her first acting role.

★ The wedding ring Michael Douglas bought for Catherine Zeta Jones came from a jewellers in Aberystwyth.

★ Christopher Reeve gained over two stone, primarily muscle, when he was first cast in the role of *Superman* in 1978.

★ Actors Gary and Martin Kemp, Pauline Quirke and Linda Robson, Gillian Taylforth and Phil Daniels were all contemporaries at the same theatre school in London.

★ *Indiana Jones* star Harrison Ford has some false teeth. A dentist pulled two of his original teeth out, while some others were damaged when he fell on a gun during a stunt for a television programme early in his career.

★ Sean Bean is permanently scarred following a fight scene with Harrison Ford in *Patriot Games*.

★ *Buffy the Vampire Slayer* actress Sarah Michelle Gellar has a brown belt in tae kwon do.

★ *Holby City's* Jeremy Edwards (Danny Shaughnessy) was known as Snoopy Boy as a child because he was always drawing Snoopy and Woodstock.

★ Richard Burton and Peter O'Toole hold the record for the most Oscar nominations without wins. Burton was nominated six times for the Best Actor prize, and once as Best Supporting Actor, while O'Toole has seven nominations for Best Actor. Albert Finney is just behind them with five nominations and no wins.

★ Arnold Schwarzenegger was considered for the title role in the 1970s TV series *The Incredible Hulk* but didn't want to do it, saying that he was too good-looking for the part.

★ As a schoolboy Robbie Coltrane was a big fan of lorries and would often pretend to be one.

★ Coltrane is known to be a good mechanic and is still a big fan of cars. Many of his friends bring their vehicles to him to be repaired.

★ *Die Hard* star Bruce Willis has to practice speaking his lines because of problems with a stutter.

★ To make Sean Connery feel more at home with James Bond's sophisticated background (which was very different to Connery's own), director Terence Young is said to have made him sleep in a Savile Row suit, complete with shirt and tie.

★ *Sex and the City's* Sarah Jessica Parker once appeared in *Shalom Sesame*, the Israeli version of Sesame Street.

★ *The Colbys* and *Bad Girls* star Stephanie Beacham has no hearing in one of her ears, and only 40 per cent hearing in the other. Her deafness was caused by her mother contracting chickenpox just days before Stephanie was born.

★ Martin Clunes first appeared on television playing a heavy glam role in *Dr Who*.

★ Gwyneth Paltrow was driving to see *Silence of the Lambs* with Steven Spielberg, when he offered her the part of Wendy in *Hook*, which launched her film career.

★ When Sylvester Stallone was attempting to sell his script for the film *Rocky* to the Hollywood studios, his only condition was that he was to play the lead role.

★ Dustin Hoffman wore a size 36C bra when playing *Tootsie*.

★ *Pearl Harbor* actress Kate Beckinsale has admitted once urinating in a director's coffee. The unnamed director had ordered Kate to strip for a nude scene, but she thought the sexy scene was unnecessary. She was so furious with him that she got her own back by adding to his flask.

★ Nicole Kidman was actually born in Honolulu, Hawaii. She didn't move to Australia until she was three.

★ Clint Eastwood is allergic to horses.

★ Macaulay Culkin made his stage debut at the tender age of four in *Bach's Babies*.

★ Former Green Cross Code man, actor David Prowse, is seen on screen as Darth Vader in *Star Wars*. He spoke all of Darth Vader's lines, and didn't know that he was going to be dubbed over by James Earl Jones until he saw the screening of the film.

★ When the film *Titanic* came out in 1997, the film's star Leonardo DiCaprio became the subject of five hundred web-sites and received six bags of fan mail a day.

★ *Friends* star Matthew Perry was offered the role of Chandler after the same American television network rejected his script for a comedy about six friends in New York.

★ Jane Seymour, the star of *Dr Quinn: Medicine Woman* has one brown eye and one green eye.

★ While filming the *Blue Lagoon*, Brooke Shields had to have her hair glued to her breasts so nothing would show.

★ Adrian and Neil Rayment, the identical twins who appeared opposite Keanu Reeves in the sci-fi blockbuster *Matrix Reloaded*, made their television debut on a *This Morning* DIY slot, and went on to co-present ITV's *Better Homes* with Carol Vorderman.

★ David Boreanaz was given the role of Angel in *Buffy the*

Vampire Slayer, after being spotted while walking his dog in Los Angeles.

★ Actress Sandra Bullock is half-Albanian and half-German.

★ Kathy Burke and *Minder* star George Cole were both fostered when they were children.

★ Bond girl Honor Blackman has a brown belt in judo.

★ Pamela Anderson was discovered when a roving arena camera focused on her as a spectator watching a Canadian football game.

★ John Travolta, Nicholas Lyndhurst and Kurt Russell are all qualified pilots.

★ Legendary actor Charles Bronson won his first movie role in *You're in the Navy Now* because of his unusual ability to belch on cue.

★ When, as a young actress, Judi Dench appeared in *Romeo and Juliet*, her proud parents reportedly watched their daughter more than seventy times. Legend goes that when, as Juliet, Judi spoke the words, 'Where is my father and my mother, Nurse?' her father replied, 'Here we are, darling, in Row H.'

★ After her Oscar nomination for *Titanic*, Kate Winslet became the youngest actress to earn two nominations (the first was for *Sense and Sensibility*).

★ Tom Cruise often learns his lines by listening to tapes because his dyslexia makes reading difficult. He also carries a dictionary around with him.

★ Cruise's facial features were used as the basis for the cartoon character of *Aladdin*.

★ During the 1980s, when members of Sinn Fein were not allowed to be heard on British television, Paul Laughran, who played Butch Dingle in *Emmerdale*, provided the voice of Gerry Adams.

★ Mel Gibson is one of eleven children.

★ *West Wing* star Rob Lowe's middle name is Helper.

★ Jim Carrey developed his comic skills by doing impersonations of his alcoholic grandparents.

★ Liz Hurley and Wendy Richard both enjoy needlepoint.

★ *Party of Five* star Jennifer Love Hewitt sent three-dozen pink roses to Gwyneth Paltrow the night before Paltrow won the Best Actress Oscar in 1999 for *Shakespeare in Love*. Hewitt also wrote her a two-page letter praising her as a role model and admiring her work. Paltrow sent a reply a week later, and Hewitt framed it.

★ Actor Rupert Everett once revealed that he had spent two years as a rent boy.

★ When he was a child, Everett used to tell everyone that Julie Andrews was his mother – his parents only realised what he was doing when people started congratulating them for bringing up Julie Andrews' son.

★ Everett also sent clippings of his pubic hair to theatregoers who complained about his performance in *The Vortex*.

★ *Thelma and Louise* star Susan Sarandon worked as a model until her first husband took her along to one of his film auditions. He failed to get a part in *Joe*, but Susan impressed the directors and won a role in the film.

★ Sarandon was temporarily banned from attending the Oscars, after protesting at the 1993 ceremony against the detention of Haitian immigrants who tested HIV-positive.

★ Clint Eastwood wore the same poncho, without ever

having washed it, in all three of his 'man with no name' western movies.

★ *Monarch of the Glen's* Archie MacDonald, actor Alistair MacKenzie, can type at 65 words per minute.

★ Movie tough guy Ray Liotta watched a heart operation in preparation for his role in *Article 99*. Unfortunately he passed out halfway through and ended up chipping two teeth and needing fifteen stitches.

★ Antonio Banderas couldn't speak English when he filmed *The Mambo Kings* in 1992, so had to perform all his lines phonetically.

★ *The Full Monty* actor Robert Carlyle was 28 when he first went abroad – his trip was to a film screening in Cannes.

★ Before being cast in the role of Rachel Green in *Friends*, Jennifer Aniston auditioned for the part of Monica, while fellow friend Courtney Cox auditioned for the role of Rachel.

★ *Forsyte Saga* star Damian Lewis used to dream about being interviewed by Terry Wogan when he was a child, but says that in his fantasy he always answered questions in an American accent.

★ Richard Kiel, who starred as Jaws in the Bond films *The Spy Who Loved Me* and *Moonraker*, is 7ft 2in tall.

★ Sharon Stone has a black belt in karate.

★ Johnny Depp only turned to acting after failing to make it in Los Angeles as a singer-guitarist.

★ Clint Eastwood wrote the theme songs to the films *Unforgiven*, *A Perfect World*, *The Bridges of Madison County* and *Absolute Power*.

★ Tamzin Outhwaite appeared in U2's video for their song 'Mysterious Ways'.

★ Although born in New York, Mel Gibson's family emigrated from the US to live in Australia when Mel was twelve because his father wanted to prevent his sons from being sent to Vietnam.

★ Corrie's Mike Baldwin, actor Johnny Briggs, once sang a duet with Hollywood movie legend Audrey Hepburn, when they appeared together in the London revue *Sauce Tartare*.

★ Actress Cameron Diaz had no acting experience when she landed the female lead alongside Jim Carrey in *The Mask*. Up until that point she had worked as a model.

★ Diaz once got alcohol poisoning in Australia at the age of eighteen.

★ *EastEnders* actress Hannah Waterman can play the tuba.

★ Paul Newman thought his performance in his first film *The Silver Chalice* was so bad that he took out an advert to apologise.

★ Bond actor Pierce Brosnan learned to be a fire-eater while he was struggling as an actor.

★ Hugh Grant and Jane Fonda can both communicate using sign language.

★ Liza Minnelli provided the voice of Dorothy in the 1964 cartoon sequel to the film that had made her mother a star – *The Wizard of Oz*. However the film, *Journey Back to Oz*, was not released until a decade later.

★ At his bodybuilding peak, Arnold Schwarzenegger's measurements were: chest 57in, waist 34in, biceps 22in, thighs 28in and calves 20in. His competition weight was 16st 11lb.

★ Demi Moore was born severely cross-eyed and had to undergo two operations as a teenager to sort out the condition.

★ Catherine Zeta Jones is named after her two grandmothers, Catherine and Zeta. Zeta was the name of the ship that her grandmother's grandfather used to sail.

★ Pierce Brosnan bought all of Ian Fleming's James Bond novels in 1986 when he was first preparing for the role of 007. The first film he ever saw was *Goldfinger*.

★ Comic actor Sir Norman Wisdom is regarded as a hero in Albania. His films were the only Western entertainment to escape censorship during the Communist era.

★ Calista Flockhart was named after her great-grandmother. Her name means 'most beautiful' in Greek.

★ Kim Basinger has a phobia of open spaces.

★ Jack Ellis, who plays the evil Fenner in *Bad Girls*, worked as a labourer for British Rail after dropping out of RADA.

★ The voice of Ursula Andress in *Dr No* was dubbed.

★ Sharon Stone always insists that there is a clause in every film contract she signs that allows her to keep all the clothes she wears during filming.

★ Former *EastEnder* Jack Ryder's middle name is Siegfried.

★ *Cold Feet* and *Fast Show* star John Thomson supplies the voice to Bill in the remake of the classic children's show, *Bill and Ben*.

★ Barbara Windsor got her first acting role after being the only person at the audition *not* to sing 'The Lady is a Tramp'.

★ Clive Dunn, who played Corporal Jones in *Dad's Army*, spent four years as a POW in Austria during the Second World War. He was captured while serving in the 4th Hussars.

★ Despite being regarded as one of cinema's greatest song-and-dance men, Fred Astaire earned his first, and only, Oscar nomination for the 1974 film *The Towering Inferno*.

FACTS ABOUT ROYALTY

Once upon a time, no one really knew what went on behind palace doors. In recent years, however, it appears that barely a week goes by without some royal revelation being reported in the papers. It seems that we cannot get enough royal gossip, so I thought it only right to include a few facts on our sovereign and her family.

★ The Duke of Edinburgh drives a black cab around London to attend engagements. He often goes unrecognised.

★ Prince Charles wears a James Bond-style waterproof alarm watch that sets off security men's pagers.

★ The Queen has thirty godchildren – one of whom is Earl Spencer, who was Princess Diana's brother.

★ Viscount Linley was the first member of the royal family to sue a newspaper when he won libel damages against *Today*.

★ One of Prince William's nicknames is Wombat, while an early nickname of Prince Philip's was Big Bubble as in 'Bubble and Squeak – Greek'.

★ Princess Margaret is the only British royal to ever to have smoked openly.

★ The Princess of Wales had to call Prince Charles 'Sir' until they were formally engaged.

★ The Queen has opened Parliament every year except 1959 and 1963, when she was expecting Prince Andrew and

Prince Edward.

★ Princess Anne was the only female competitor in the Montreal Olympics of 1976 not to be given a sex test.

★ The names of the Queen's corgis are Pharos, Emma, Swift and Linnet.

★ Viscount Linley was the first member of the royal family to ever be banned from driving.

★ The Duchess of York had to tone down her posh accent after a commercial for cranberry juice confused many viewers, who couldn't understand a word she was saying.

★ The Queen has given out over 75,000 Christmas puddings to staff since the start of her reign.

★ Following their family tree, William and Harry's surname should be Schleswig-Holstein-Sonderburg-Glucksburg-Saxe-Coburg-Gotha.

★ The Queen has introduced a new breed of dog to Britain. Known as the 'dorgi', it was produced when one of her corgis mated with a dachshund belonging to Princess Margaret.

★ The first football match the Queen attended was the 1953 FA Cup final.

★ Prince Andrew was rather mischievous as a child. He is said to have put itching powder in the Queen's bed and changed the signs around at a Buckingham Palace garden party.

★ Unusual live gifts given to the Queen on foreign tours include two tortoises, a seven-year-old bull elephant called Jumbo, beavers, sloths and a canary.

★ President Tubman of Liberia gave two hippopotami to the Duke of Edinburgh in 1961.

★ Prince Andrew was presented with a baby crocodile called

Mansa following the Queen's state visit to the Gambia in the early 1960s.

★ Four days before her coronation in 1953, the Queen embarked on a special diet of hard-boiled eggs and salt, which were said to prevent her becoming hungry or needing to go to the toilet during the long coronation ceremony.

★ Anti-smoker Prince Charles once reportedly bet Camilla Parker Bowles £50 that she could not give up the weed. Camilla was keen to give up her habit at the time, and so accepted the bet. Charles discovered that he had unfortunately won the bet, however, when a Sunday newspaper published a photograph of Camilla smoking while out hunting.

★ The Duke of Edinburgh was fifty when he retired from playing polo.

★ Princess Anne learned to ride horses when she was two and a half.

★ The Duke of Edinburgh was the first member of the Royal Family to be interviewed on television, in May 1961.

★ Princess Anne holds an HGV licence.

★ When Prince Charles was studying at Cambridge, he gained University Colours – a half-Blue, for polo.

★ The Queen has made a Christmas broadcast to the Commonwealth every year of her reign except 1969, when a repeat of the film *Royal Family* was shown instead. The previous year was the last time her Christmas message was broadcast live.

★ Although Prince Philip is known as being Greek royalty, he does not speak any Greek and has no Greek blood in him. He actually belongs to the Danish royal family, who took over the monarchy of Greece.

★ Prince Edward was nicknamed 'Jaws' at school because of the braces he wore on his teeth.

★ The Duke of Edinburgh was the first royal to broadcast from a television studio. In May 1957 he presented a programme called *Round the World in Forty Minutes* in which he talked about his journey around the globe the previous year aboard the Royal yacht *Britannia*.

★ When he was younger, Prince William spent many hours in his bedroom learning to moonwalk like Michael Jackson.

★ Prince Edward is regarded as the cleverest of the Queen's children, having passed nine O levels and three A levels.

★ Princess Anne was the first daughter of a sovereign to attend boarding school.

★ Prince Harry receives so much mail from young girls asking him out that he needs two secretaries to help him out.

★ The Queen Mother, who died in 2002 at the age of 101, lived longer than any other king or queen in British history.

★ The Queen Mother always dressed for dinner – whether there were guests or not.

★ The Queen is the only person in Britain legally allowed to eat swan.

★ Princess Anne's nose was the most popular model for women wanting plastic surgery in the 1970s.

★ The Queen employs around three hundred servants, while Prince Charles 85.

★ Prince Andrew was often kept out of the public eye when he was a child, leading the press to speculate that he had some mental disability.

★ Prince Philip is said to have been born on a dining-room table.

★ Prince Charles owns a collection of toilet seats.

★ Before she married Prince Edward, Sophie Rhys-Jones worked in PR, where one of her clients was Mr Blobby.

★ A grain of rice with a portrait of the Queen and the Duke of Edinburgh engraved on it was once insured at Lloyd's for $20,000.

★ Other boys may get a cheque from their grandmother for their eighteenth birthday, but not Prince Harry. The Queen marked the occasion by presenting him with his own coat of arms.

★ Because of Prince Edward's size at birth (5lb 11oz), the Royal Family had expected a girl. The Queen had chosen only female names.

FACTS ABOUT FAMOUS
POLITICIANS

★ ★ ★ ★ ★ ★ ★ ★ ★ ★ ★ ★ ★

They have more power than Jeremy Clarkson's car, and more responsibility than the school milk monitor. They are the people who make the decisions that decide how the country is run.

But are our politicians really up to the job?

★ Former Liberal leader Paddy Ashdown is a qualified Chinese interpreter.

★ Former US President Gerald Ford was one of the members of the Warren Commission, which was appointed to study the assassination of John F Kennedy.

★ When Gordon Brown was 21, he entered and won a *Daily Express* competition for his vision of Britain in the year 2000. He wrote of 'a society where government enables people to fulfil their abilities and aspirations'.

★ John Major is Margaret Thatcher's fifth cousin once removed.

★ In 1969, Margaret Thatcher declared that 'no woman will be prime minister in my lifetime'.

★ Before becoming an MP, former Speaker of the House of Commons Betty Boothroyd worked on John F Kennedy's election campaign.

★ Former Russian President Boris Yeltsin worked on a construction site before moving into politics.

★ Labour politician David Blunkett's guide dog is called Sadie.

★ One of Blunkett's earlier guide dogs was once sick in the House of Commons debating chamber.

★ Tony Blair started dating his future wife Cherie Booth after passing a balloon between his knees to hers at a Christmas party.

★ Former Tory leader William Hague is colour-blind.

★ In 1966, British diplomats were so concerned with a young Jack Straw on a visit to Chile, they cabled London to warn foreign office officials that he was a 'troublemaker ... acting with malice'. At the time Straw was a left-wing student leader, whom diplomats thought could damage Anglo-Chile relations.

★ While prime minister in the late 1960s, Harold Wilson sued pop group The Move for the promotional artwork for their song 'Flowers in the Rain' which featured him in a compromising position. All royalties from the song went to charity.

★ Bill Clinton is allergic to flowers.

★ President George Bush once gave Chinese Premier Li Peng a pair of cowboy boots. The sole of one boot displayed the Chinese flag, with the Stars and Stripes on the other. Unfortunately, in Asia the sole of the foot is considered the lowliest, dirtiest part of the body.

★ World War II Prime Minister Winston Churchill had a stutter as a child. One of his teachers warned, 'Because of his stuttering he should be discouraged from following in his father's political footsteps.'

★ While at university, Tony Blair was accused of entertaining young ladies in his room late at night, after an incriminating lipstick was discovered. Blair declared that the lipstick was his.

★ Labour MP Bob Cryer was the first MP to speak from the televised House of Commons in 1989.

★ Long before he punched a voter during the 2001 general election campaign, John Prescott was nicknamed 'Thumper' by his friends, for his readiness to give enemies a verbal pounding when they caused him to lose his temper.

★ George W Bush is the second president to follow in his father's footsteps. The first father and son presidents were John Adams and John Quincy Adams.

★ Paddy Ashdown's grandfather was the first man in Ireland to buy a car.

★ Mo Mowlam was tipped to become the first female prime minister by her tutors at Durham University.

★ Mowlam only has one Christian name – Marjorie – because when her father went to register her birth, he couldn't remember the second name her mother had chosen for her. As a child, it annoyed her that her brother and sister both had two Christian names.

★ Ann Widdecombe is such an animal lover that when her two black cats died a fortnight after each other, she wrote a eulogy in a national newspaper.

★ Ronald Reagan was nicknamed 'Dutch' because, when his father first saw him, he said he looked like a fat little Dutchman.

★ Reagan used to keep a jar of jellybeans on his desk.

★ Tony Blair used to play in a group called Ugly Rumours.

★ Former Labour leader Neil Kinnock and shadow chancellor Michael Howard were also budding rock'n'roll stars in their youth. They both played in skiffle groups.

★ US President John F Kennedy could speed-read 2,000 words per minute.

★ Bill Clinton met JFK when he was seventeen.

★ After being shot, Kennedy was admitted to Parkland Memorial Hospital, Dallas as 'Patient 24740 – White Male'.

★ While at school, Labour MP Robin Cook always wore two badges on his blazer. One supported the anti-apartheid movement, the other backed CND.

★ Margaret Thatcher was the only female member of Edward Heath's cabinet when he first became prime minister in 1970.

★ Tony Benn first became an MP aged 25.

★ Gordon Brown was only nineteen when he achieved a First in History from Edinburgh University.

★ George W Bush gave up alcohol the day after his fortieth birthday. It is rumoured that his wife had issued him with an ultimatum – it was either her or Jack Daniels.

★ Despite being known as a Yorkshireman, John Prescott was actually born in Prestatyn in Wales. He didn't move to South Yorkshire until he was five years old.

★ Libyan leader Colonel Gadaffi is said to enjoy reading Barbara Cartland novels.

★ Bill Clinton was actually born William Blythe. His natural father died in a car accident before he was born, and his mother remarried Roger Clinton when Bill was four.

★ Margaret Thatcher's office once proposed to Buckingham Palace that they co-ordinate the colours of outfits when the two women would be appearing together in public. Buckingham Palace replied that this was unnecessary, as the Queen never noticed what Mrs Thatcher was wearing anyway.

★ John Major, the former prime minister, suffers from hay fever.

★ Former chancellor Denis Healey was the only real person to appear on the satirical show *Spitting Image*.

★ When the Clintons left the White House, they packed up over fifty recent gifts from political supporters. Among the presents (which had a combined worth of $190,027), was a golf driver valued at $350 from Jack Nicholson and boxing gloves worth $300 from Sylvester Stallone.

★ Ann Widdecombe converted to Catholicism in protest over Anglican ordination of women.

★ Roy Hattersley was the youngest ever leader of Sheffield City Council. He was just 25 when he took charge.

★ When Hattersley pulled out of an appearance on the satirical quiz show *Have I Got News For You* in 1993, he was replaced on the programme by a tub of lard. Panellist Paul Merton declared, 'They possess the same qualities and are liable to give similar performances.'

★ Former disgraced American President Richard Nixon, worried about his grades while at Duke University Law School, broke into the dean's office to find his records, which actually showed he was top of his class.

★ When Prime Minister Harold Wilson entered Downing Street for the first time in 1964, the first meal he ate there was fish fingers.

FACTS ABOUT OTHER FAMOUS PEOPLE

These facts are a random selection about other famous people from all walks of life who don't fit into any of the categories that have been featured so far.

★ Microsoft founder Bill Gates has a photographic memory.

★ In Japan, David Beckham, or 'Bekkamu' as he is known, has name recognition of more than 90 per cent, a feat only usually achieved by film stars or musicians.

★ Long before he married Posh Spice, Beckham snogged Atomic Kitten's Jenny Frost.

★ Children's author Roald Dahl wrote his novel, *The BFG*, for his model granddaughter Sophie Dahl.

★ Helena Christensen was named after Helen of Troy, a woman whose beauty started a war.

★ Songwriter Burt Bacharach, whose writing partnership with Hal David was one of the most successful of all time, actually scored his first hit as a composer with Hal's brother, Mack David. The piece was the Five Blobs' 'The Blob', which was written for a horror B-movie.

★ *Gladiator* director Ridley Scott was responsible for the Hovis advert, which featured the delivery boy and the cobbled hill. He also worked on the 1960s police series *Z Cars*.

★ When she was a teenager, Cherie Booth told a friend that she wanted to be Britain's first female prime minister.

★ Booth got the highest-scoring first degree in her year from the London School of Economics. She also topped the year in the 1976 bar exams.

★ *Ready Steady Cook* regular James Martin cooked for the Queen Mother when he was only twelve years old. His father ran the catering at Castle Howard in Yorkshire, and the future celebrity chef helped prepare the meal for the royal guest during her visit to the stately home.

★ Lord Robert Winston, one of the world's foremost experts in IVF treatment, and presenter of many BBC programmes, worked as a theatre director in the 1960s.

★ *I'm a Celebrity ... Get Me Out of Here* 2003 runner-up John Fashanu was brought up by Barnardos and later by foster parents.

★ Record producer Pete Waterman only learned to read properly at the age of 38.

★ Writer Virginia Woolf, who was portrayed by Oscar winner Nicole Kidman in *The Hours*, wrote all of her books standing up.

★ Snooker player Jimmy White was the first person to start the National Lottery balls rolling using a snooker cue, when he appeared on the programme in 1997. That night's jackpot of £4.7 million was won by a South Wales snooker-team syndicate.

★ Tara Palmer-Tomkinson once played a concert recital in Belfast. She has also appeared in a Puff Daddy video with Danny de Vito and Dennis Hopper.

★ Walt Disney was the first film producer to appear on a US postage stamp.

★ Director James Cameron drew all of Jack's pictures in *Titanic*. He also drew the picture of Rose on the couch – the hands you see in the film are his.

★ Professor Stephen Hawking was diagnosed with a form of motor neurone disease just before his 21st birthday, while he was in his final year as an Oxford undergraduate. At the time, over forty years ago, he was given just two years to live.

★ Serial killer Charles Manson auditioned for the Monkees.

★ Thriller writer Frederick Forsyth became a bullfighter at seventeen, while at nineteen he became the youngest pilot in the Royal Air Force.

★ Unlike Alfred Hitchcock, director Steven Spielberg rarely makes an appearance in his own films. He is almost seen, however, in *The Lost World: Jurassic Park*. His reflection can be made out eating popcorn while sitting next to star Jeff Goldblum during the CNN television story about dinosaurs.

★ Spoon-bender Uri Geller was a pupil of Salvador Dali's for two years and is an accomplished artist. He served in the Israeli army as a paratrooper and fought in the Six Day War.

★ *Only Fools and Horses* creator John Sullivan used to work as a sceneshifter for the BBC.

★ When she was fourteen years old, Jerry Hall reportedly told her mother, 'I'm going to be the richest, best known and most beautiful model in the world.'

★ Many years before he found himself on the wrong side of the law, novelist and disgraced former MP Jeffrey Archer trained as a police officer.

★ After working with many famous chefs, including Marco Pierre White and Albert Roux, Gordon Ramsy took a year off at the age of 26 to cook on media tycoon Reg Grundy's yacht. Grundy's company makes *Neighbours*.

★ As a boy, Terry Venables was a member of a song-and-dance

troupe called 'The Happy Tappers'.

★ Gold-medal-winning heptathlete Denise Lewis was so focused as a child that her primary school teachers predicted she would end up as prime minister.

★ Director Guy Ritchie is dyslexic and struggled through school. He left with only one qualification – a GCSE in film studies.

★ Terry Waite has size 14 feet.

★ After being crowned Miss Denmark when she was eighteen, supermodel Helena Christiansen joined the hippie trail. She only stumbled into modelling because she needed the money.

★ Trevor Bayliss, inventor of the wind-up radio, actually failed his eleven-plus.

★ As a young boy Frankie Dettori had his heart set on a football career, but after receiving a pony for his sixth birthday he turned his attention to horse racing.

★ Chef and restaurateur Raymond Blanc has never had a formal cookery lesson.

★ Alfred Hitchcock didn't have a bellybutton. It disappeared when he was sewn up after surgery.

★ Although he has a reputation as being a hot-headed chef, Gordon Ramsay says he does not treat others as badly as he was treated himself by his former boss Joel Robouchon. On his first day, Ramsay is said to have messed up a langoustine ravioli. Robouchon threw the lot, which was still burning hot, over Ramsay's head.

★ 'King of the Jungle' Phil Tufnell retired from first-class cricket just so he could take part in *I'm a Celebrity ... Get Me Out of Here*. He had asked his County for time off to take up the challenge, but they refused.

★ While studying theology at Cambridge University, the current Archbishop of Canterbury, Rowan Williams, was torn between Roman Catholicism and Anglicanism. He eventually chose the latter.

★ In the 2002 general election, model Jordan stood as a candidate for the Greater Manchester constituency of Stretford and Urmston. Her manifesto pledge included the promise of free plastic surgery for all.

★ Director Quentin Tarantino was still working in a video-rental store right up to the filming of *Reservoir Dogs*. He was prepared to make the film for just $10,000 before actor Harvey Keitel agreed to act as executive producer, which led to the budget increasing to $1.5 million.

★ JK Rowling came up with the idea for Harry Potter while on a train journey from London to Edinburgh.

★ The café where Rowling wrote the first Harry Potter book is called Nicholson's Café. Her brother-in-law owns it.

★ Film director and restaurant critic Michael Winner was a boarder at a Quaker school, where he was only allowed to eat vegetarian food.

CELEBRITY AGES

I had planned to write a section on how old celebrities really are, but realised it would be an impossible task – many famous people lie about their age so often that even they don't know how many candles should go on their birthday cake.

So instead, this section is a mixture of those famous people who have either achieved something notable at a particularly young age, as well as those whose achievements are noted because of their more mature years, along with a few celebrities who were born on the same day (some ageing a lot better than others!).

★ Bjork had a platinum-selling album in Iceland at the age of eleven.

★ Joan Collins was fifty when she graced the centrefold of *Playboy*.

★ Arnold Schwarzenegger was named Mr Universe when he was just twenty.

★ Ricky Martin joined the Puerto Rican boy band Menudo when he was twelve.

★ Lulu sang for the first time in public when she was four.

★ *Red Dwarf* star Craig Charles was winning awards as a poet at the age of twelve.

★ *Lord of the Rings* star Sir Ian McKellen performed his first play (Shakespeare's *Twelfth Night*) when he was thirteen.

★ *Lord of the Rings* director Peter Jackson made his first film when he was twelve. The film was about World War II. He and a couple of friends dug a hole in the garden, and demonstrated an early interest in special effects by making holes in the celluloid to simulate gunshots.

★ Richard Dreyfuss is the youngest man ever to win the Best Actor Oscar. He won it in 1977 for *The Goodbye Girl*, when he was 29 years and 156 days. He was just over a year younger than Marlon Brando, who was 30 years and 361 days when he won the same award in 1954 for *On the Waterfront*.

★ At the other end of the scale is Henry Fonda, who takes the title of the oldest person to win the Best Actor Oscar. He was 76 years and 317 days when won the award for his performance in *On Golden Pond* in 1981.

★ Jessica Tandy remains the oldest woman to pick up the Oscar for Best Actress. She was 80 years and 293 days when she won the award in 1989 for *Driving Miss Daisy*.

★ *Wizard of Oz* star Judy Garland appeared in her first film at the age of seven. She had made 28 films by the time she was 26.

★ TV chef Jamie Oliver started cooking at his father's pub when he was eight.

★ Bill Gates wrote his first computer program when he was thirteen, at a time when computers were still the size of rooms and run by scientists in white coats.

★ Stevie Wonder was eleven years old when he signed his first recording contract with Motown.

★ Singer LeAnn Rimes was just thirteen years old when she won two Grammy awards. She continues to hold the record for the longest-running single on the *Billboard* top 100 – 'How Do I Live?'

★ Michael J Fox was almost thirty years old when he made his last appearance as time-travelling teenager Marty McFly in *Back to the Future III*.

★ Dustin Hoffman was also thirty when he played the 21-year-old Benjamin Braddock in *The Graduate*.

★ Drew Barrymore made her acting debut aged just eleven months, in an advert for dog food.

★ Actress Whoopi Goldberg became a grandmother when she was 35.

★ Comedian Frank Skinner was 44 before he ever had a swimming lesson. He still can't ride a bike or ice-skate.

★ *Question Time* presenter David Dimbleby made his broadcasting debut at the age of twelve, when he compered the Boxing Day edition of the popular programme *Family Favourites*.

★ Actress Penelope Keith and soul star Marvin Gaye were born on the same day (2 April 1939).

★ Suggs (January 1961), Christopher Plummer (December 1929) and Zoë Wanamaker (May 1949) were all born on Friday 13th.

★ Michael Douglas (born 25 September 1944) is exactly 25 years older than his wife Catherine Zeta Jones (born 25 September 1969).

★ Singers Peter Gabriel and Stevie Wonder were born on the same day (13 May 1950).

★ David Frost and film director Francis Ford Coppola were born on the same day (7 April 1939).

★ Leslie Ash and Prince Andrew were born on the same day (19 February 1960).

CELEBRITY MONEY

As well as being a nation obsessed with celebrity, we are also a nation obsessed with money. Although we don't like to talk about how much we earn, we are always passing comment on how much we think other people are raking in.

Some famous people would need several months to work out exactly how much they were worth now. However, it is interesting to note that they were not always so flush.

★ Sean Connery was paid £6,000 to star in the first James Bond film *Dr No*.

★ David Bowie's first recorded wage was £147, for a tour. Years later, his 'Glass Spider Tour' made him £15 million.

★ Before they hit the big time, the Spice Girls earned just £60 a week.

★ Comedian and quiz-show host extraordinaire Bob Monkhouse sold his first jokes to fellow comedian Max Miller for just five shillings when he was sixteen years old.

★ The original celebrity aerobic goddess, Jane Fonda, grossed £700 million from her exercise videos.

★ John Cleese and Connie Booth earned just £1,000 per episode for writing the comedy classic *Fawlty Towers*. The series was sold to television networks worldwide, and went on to become one of the biggest-selling BBC videos of all time.

★ When Prince Philip proposed to the then Princess Elizabeth, he was in the navy and earning just £9 per week.

★ When Jamie Oliver first started working at his dad's pub in Essex, he was paid £7.50 for two afternoons' work. He was still so hard up when he asked his girlfriend Jools to marry him that he couldn't afford to buy her a ring for three years.

★ Marlon Brando received $4 million for his ten minutes of screen time in *Superman*.

★ Michael Jackson earned £200 per second during his 1988 world tour.

★ Aged 22, Angus Deayton sold his first script to comedian Dick Emery for £40.

★ Jonathan Ross sold his successful production company, Channel X, for just £1.

★ Shamed former Tory MP Jonathan Aitken earned just £5.60 per week as a prison lavatory cleaner, while serving his sentence for perjury. He had previously enjoyed life as a multimillionaire.

★ *Carry On* stalwart Kenneth Williams earned £800 for his role in the first *Carry On* film in 1958, *Carry On Sergeant*. His fee stayed the same until 1962 when it was raised to £5,000, the same as fellow performer Sid James.

★ Naomi Campbell earned £100,000 for allowing Madonna to suck her toe in a photo shoot for Madonna's book *Sex*.

★ In 1968, when Elton John and song-writing partner Bernie Taupin were signed by Dick James to be staff writers for his new company DJM Records, they were paid just £10 per week.

★ Tom Jones's first job was in a glove factory, where he earned just £2 per week.

★ Terry Wogan earned £35 per programme when he joined the

BBC in 1967 to present *Late Night Extra* on the new Radio 1 and 2 every Wednesday evening.

★ When Elizabeth Taylor starred in *Lassie Come Home*, she was paid $100 a week, while the dog received $250.

Once they have earned a lot of money, it seems only right that the celebrities should then spend it.

★ Actor Arnold Schwarzenegger paid $772,500 for President John F Kennedy's golf clubs at a 1996 auction.

★ Arnie is also believed to have paid a massive $38 million for a Gulfstream Jet in 1997.

★ Television presenter and Stoke City fan Nick Hancock paid £20,000 for Sir Stanley Matthews' 1953 FA Cup winners medal.

★ Chris Evans wooed wife-to-be Billie Piper with a £110,000 Ferrari, which he covered with red roses and balloons. She didn't have a driving licence at the time.

★ Comedian David Baddiel paid £3,000 for one of Charles Dickens' business cards.

★ Frank Skinner paid £11,200 in 1997 for a blue velvet shirt, which was worn by Elvis Presley in 1956.

★ George Michael once splashed out £17,000 on a haircut.

★ Pete Waterman once bought eighteen Ferraris in one go and became the first man to buy a part of the privatised British Rail. He also once owned the legendary locomotive *The Flying Scotsman*.

★ Elton John famously admitted spending £293,000 on flowers, while in one twenty-month period he spent £40 million on clothes, cars, art and travels. He is believed to have forked out

£300,000 on spectacles during his career.

★ Elton also spent £6 million on his beloved Watford Football Club. He later sold his interest in the club for only £2 million.

★ Known for his generosity towards friends, Elton once bought fellow singer Kiki Dee a ring worth over £15,000 just because she was feeling a bit unhappy.

★ Blue star Lee Ryan paid £10,000 for a white sequinned suit owned by Elton John. The Mozart-style suit was part of Sir Elton's sale of 20,000 items to raise money for AIDS charities.

★ Comedian and *Jonathan Creek* star Alan Davies paid £35,000 at auction to secure the diary-room chair from the original *Big Brother*. He beat a bid from disqualified contestant 'Nasty' Nick Bateman.

★ Pierce Brosnan bought the typewriter of the James Bond creator, Ian Fleming, for £52,800.

★ American actor Ben Affleck demonstrated his love for Jennifer Lopez by splashing out £250,000 on a blue Bentley for her.

★ P Diddy spent £1.7 million on the video for 'Victory', making it the second-most expensive video ever behind Michael Jackson's 'Thriller'. The shoot included the blowing up of a 747 aircraft, which alone cost £38,000.

★ After signing his first professional contract with Manchester United when he was eighteen, David Beckham bought a Ford Escort from his team-mate Ryan Giggs.

★ Later on in his career, when he was earning rather more, Beckham spent a reported £11,000 on yellow roses for his future wife Victoria. He sent her one rose every day from the day they met until they started living together.

★ Keanu Reeves bought twelve stuntmen a £10,000 motorbike

each, as a parting gift after shooting the film *Matrix Reloaded*.

On the other hand, some celebrities tend to be more cautious and spend their money insuring their assets.

★ Hollywood actress Betty Grable began the trend in the 1940s when she insured her legs for $1 million.

★ *Lord of the Dance* star Michael Flatley is said to have his legs insured for £25 million.

★ Meanwhile, fellow dancing legend Fred Astaire insured his for the more modest sum of $75,000 each.

★ Actress Jamie Lee Curtis took out a £1 million insurance policy to cover her legs while taking part in an advertising campaign for a stocking company.

★ Rolling Stones drummer Keith Richards has insured his hands for £1 million.

★ England captain Alan Shearer's £15 million transfer fee meant that in 1996 he had to fly on a separate plane from the rest of the Newcastle United team, as the travel insurance was too high.

★ Dolly Parton reportedly has her breasts insured for $600,000.

★ Ken Dodd's trademark teeth are insured for £4 million.

★ Cricketer Merv Hughes once took out a £200,000 policy on his distinctive handlebar moustache.

★ American singer Bruce Springsteen insured his voice for $6 million – Rod Stewart does the same.

★ While he was still fighting, boxer Nigel Benn had his fists insured for £10 million.

★ Several years ago, gourmet and food critic Egon Ronay insured his taste buds for £250,000.

★ Marilyn Monroe is believed to have been the first star to be insured against drug use. Three American film studios purchased policies to protect against losses if the star's drug use interfered with filming schedules.

★ In 1989, newspapers reported that Jimmy Saville had his legs insured for £1 million against injury in the London Marathon.

MEMORABILIA OF THE RICH AND FAMOUS

Almost any object in some way connected with a well-known star can be collectable, from items of clothing and autographs, to rare photographs and even samples of nasal hair. Collectors pay particularly high prices for the musical instruments upon which a star once performed.

★ John Lennon's Rolls-Royce Phantom V was sold in 1985 for an incredible $2.3 million, while a photograph of John Lennon's spectacles, bloodstained from when he was shot dead, was sold for nearly £9,000 in 2002. The image was taken by Yoko Ono and is one of only six such prints in existence.

★ Geri Halliwell's Union Jack dress, which she wore at the Brits in 1997, made £41,320 at an auction in 1998.

★ Eric Clapton's 'Brownie' guitar, which he played on the recording of 'Layla', sold at auction in 1999 for £316,879.

★ A manuscript by 'beat generation' writer Jack Kerouac sold for £1.5 million at auction in 2001. His typed draft of *On the Road*, on a continuous 120ft roll, was sold at Christie's.

★ An empty mineral water bottle, signed by Madonna and smudged with her lipstick, made £446 at auction.

★ Actor Marlon Brando's costume, which he wore for the film *Mutiny on the Bounty*, sold for £6,940 in 1997.

★ A collection of letters and cards sent by Diana, Princess of Wales, to a former housekeeper at her childhood home, sold for £22,000 at auction in 2002. The letters and cards were sent to Maud Pendrey, who was in her seventies and was a housekeeper at Diana's family home at Althrop, near Northampton.

★ A pair of ruby slippers worn by Judy Garland in the *Wizard of Oz*, were sold at auction for $660,000 in 2000. The size 6B shoes, or 4 1/2 as they are known in the UK, were bought by a private collector.

★ Bill Clinton's signed saxophone fetched £22,000 at auction in 1994.

★ Jimi Hendrix's Fender Stratocaster, which he used at Woodstock in 1969, was sold in 1990 for £198,000.

★ A four-inch strand of Bob Marley's dreadlocked hair sold for £2,585 in 2003.

★ The lock was cut off by the star and given to a girl he had met after a concert in London in 1980, a year before he died of cancer.

★ Elton John's 1998 auction of clothes, furniture and other possessions, took three days to complete and raised £4,838,022.

★ Charlton Heston's loin cloth, from the film *Ben-Hur*, raised £6,250 at auction in 1997.

★ A Knabe grand piano once owned by Elvis Presley sold for £430,000 in 2003. Presley used it until 1969 when his wife, Priscilla Presley, gave him a new Steinway piano.

★ Meanwhile, clippings of Elvis's jet-black hair sold in a 2002 US auction for nearly £73,000. The hair was collected by the star's former barber Homer Gilleland and kept in a jar with a vacuum seal.

★ A two-line handwritten quotation from a Beatles' song

fetched £1,350 at auction. The note, from Paul McCartney to an old family friend, quoted the opening lines of his penned 1967 hit 'Penny Lane'.

★ In 1999, the dress that Marilyn Monroe wore when she breathlessly sang 'Happy Birthday' to President Kennedy in 1962, broke records when it fetched $1,267,500 at auction. The flesh-coloured dress, so tight she had to be sewn into it, had originally cost $12,000. At the same auction a pair of glass slippers, originally estimated to sell for up to $1,500, went for $90,500.

CELEBRITIES IN A LATHER

If celebrities are our new neighbours, then the characters in soap operas are our new family. We see them more often than many members of our family, they are always in our homes, and we know more about their lives than we do about some of our supposed nearest and dearest. We talk about them in pubs and treat them as if they were real people.

In the four decades and more since *Coronation Street* first hit our screens, more than a few future stars have entered the world of the 'serial drama', many of them starring in more than one soap.

★ David Jason once had a small role playing a gardener in *Crossroads*.

★ Robbie Williams made a brief appearance in *EastEnders* in 1995. He was an extra in the background of a scene in the Queen Vic.

★ Sarah Lancashire made her first appearance in *Coronation Street* in 1987, playing a nurse called Wendy Farmer who applied to be the Duckworth's lodger. It was another four years before she returned as barmaid Raquel Wolstenhulme.

★ Beverly Callard made an appearance in *Emmerdale* before going on to play Liz MacDonald in *Coronation Street*. She played one of Jackie Merrick's girlfriends – Angie Richards.

★ Just before she found fame as *Brooksides'* Sheila Grant, *Royle Family* actress Sue Johnston appeared in *Coronation*

Street as bookie's wife Mrs Chadwick.

★ Singer and musical star Michael Ball also made an early appearance in *Coronation Street*. His character, Malcolm Nuttall, had a fight with Kevin Webster over a girl.

★ Letitia Dean may be best known to *EastEnders* viewers, but she got her break in *Brookside,* playing a character called Dawn in 1984.

★ Eileen Derbyshire, who plays Emily Bishop in *Coronation Street*, is the longest serving actress in any soap in the world. She first appeared in episode fifteen of the soap in January 1961.

★ Before he made his name as a Professional, actor Martin Shaw appeared in *Coronation Street* as a hippy student called Robert Croft.

★ Derek Martin had several chances to join the *EastEnders* cast before joining the soap as Charlie Slater. He turned down the role of Frank Butcher and even auditioned for the part of Den Watts.

★ Kelvin Fletcher, who plays Andy Sugden in *Emmerdale*, once made a brief appearance in *Coronation Street*. He rode his bike past Deirdre as she mourned the death of husband Samir Rachid on the canal towpath.

★ Former Hear'say member, Kym Marsh, once had a walk-on role in *EastEnders*. She was part of a crowd drinking outside the Queen Vic, while Sonia and Jamie (Kym's real-life husband Jack Ryder) had a row.

★ Before he became a member of 60s boy band the Monkees, Davy Jones appeared in *Coronation Street* as the grandson of soap battle-axe Ena Sharples.

★ Laurence Olivier was such a fan of Hilda Ogden that he

joined forces with Michael Parkinson and Russell Harty to form the Hilda Ogden Appreciation Society.

★ Olivier actually agreed to play a tramp in *Coronation Street*, but had to back out at the last minute because of other filming commitments.

★ Brooke Kinsella auditioned for the parts of Janine Butcher, Sonia Jackson and Zoe Slater in *EastEnders*, before finally being given the part of stallholder Kelly.

★ Paul McKenna appeared as a hypnotist in *Hollyoaks* in 2000, performing at a theme night at The Dog.

★ Alan Fletcher may be known today as Ramsey Street's Dr Karl Kennedy, however he first appeared in *Neighbours* in the late 80s as Greg Cooper.

★ Sue Nicholls, who plays *Coronation Street's* Audrey Roberts, is married in real life to actor Mark Eden, who appeared in the soap as baddie Alan Bradley.

★ Nicholls auditioned for the role of Jill Richardson in *Crossroads*, but failed to get it, as the Brummie accent she put on was considered to be too strong.

★ Actor and television globetrotter Michael Palin once made a brief appearance in *Home and Away*. He played a lost surfer who stopped off at the diner to ask the way to the beach.

★ *Holby City* heart-throb Jeremy Sheffield made his television debut delivering crisps to the Queen Vic in *EastEnders*.

★ Mona Hammond, who played Blossom Jackson in *EastEnders*, was the midwife who delivered Vicki Fowler in 1986.

★ Clive Hornby is not the only person to play Jack Sugden in *Emmerdale*. Although the character appeared in the first episode of the soap in 1972, Andrew Burt originally played Jack.

★ Barbara Windsor did not always play *EastEnders'* Peggy Mitchell. Actress Jo Warne was originally cast in the role.

★ Meanwhile, fellow *EastEnders* character Janine Butcher has been seen in three different incarnations. Rebecca Michael, Alexia Demetriou and Charlie Brooks have all played Frank Butcher's daughter.

★ The character of Max Cunningham in *Hollyoaks* was originally played by actor Ben Sherrif before Matt Littler took over the role.

★ Before making her name as lesbian Beth Jordache in *Brookside*, actress Anna Friel had had small roles in both *Emmerdale* and *Coronation Street*.

★ Sarah Lancashire's dad Geoffrey was a scriptwriter on *Coronation Street* before his daughter joined the cast as Raquel.

★ Paula Tilbrook, who is now known as Betty Eagleton in *Emmerdale*, once made an appearance in Corrie, as a woman who had a crush on Alf Roberts.

★ Nicholas Bailey, now best known as *EastEnders'* Dr Trueman, appeared in *Coronation Street* as the brother of hairdresser Fiona Middleton.

★ *EastEnders'* Laura Beale, actress Hannah Waterman, originally appeared in the soap two years before she joined the cast full time. She was seen in one episode as a character called Maria.

★ *Heartbeat*'s Gina Ward, actress Tricia Penrose, has done the rounds of the soaps. Aged fourteen she played Damon Grant's girlfriend Ruth in *Brookside*, and later played WPC Emma Reid, whose affair with Rod Corkhill ended his engagement to Kirsty

Brown. She also appeared as Elsa Feldman's friend in *Emmerdale*, before turning up in *Coronation Street* as a hotel receptionist for Ken Barlow and Alma Sedgewick.

★ Many years before he was annoying Rita in 'The Kabin', Malcolm Hebden, who plays Corrie's Norris Cole, played a Spanish waiter called Carlos who proposed to Mavis.

★ Clive James was seen but not heard in an episode of *Neighbours*. He played a postman.

★ Shane Richie originally auditioned for the role of Tom the fireman in *Eastenders*, before being cast as lovable rogue Alfie Moon.

★ Although best known as *Home and Away* stalwart Donald Fisher, actor Norman Coburn once appeared in *Coronation Street*.

★ June Brown got the role of Dot Cotton in *EastEnders* having been spotted in an episode of *Minder* by Leslie Grantham, who was then appearing in the soap as Den Watts.

★ Before finding worldwide fame as a Spice Girl, Melanie Brown appeared as an extra in *Emmerdale*. Her sister Danielle also featured in the soap, and was seen cleaning chalets at the holiday village.

★ Richard Thorpe, who plays *Emmerdale*'s Alan Turner, once spent a year at the *Crossroads* motel, where he appeared as a sailor.

★ Noddy Holder, of Slade fame, once made a brief appearance in *Coronation Street* as Stan Potter.

★ Amanda Holden had her acting break in 1985 in an episode of *EastEnders* playing a stallholder called Carmen. She has said that the day she left Walford, she slipped a note under the producer's door suggesting Carmen should come back and that the audience should learn her surname is Getme.

★ Since leaving Albert Square, actress Susan Tully, who played *EastEnders'* Michelle Fowler, has been working on the other side of the camera. As well as directing episodes of *EastEnders*, she has also produced episodes of *The Bill*.

★ Two actors have played the part of *EastEnders'* Martin Fowler. Jon Peyton-Price was originally cast in the role, but in December 1996 the character of Martin was recast, with James Alexandrou in the role.

★ Television presenter Cat Deeley played the mystery girl who sailed off into the sunset with Finn in *Hollyoaks*.

★ *Dalziel and Pascoe* star Warren Clarke has appeared in six episodes of *Coronation Street*, playing three different characters.

★ Hollywood actor Ben Kingsley, who won a Best Actor Oscar for the film *Gandhi*, appeared in *Coronation Street* during the 1960s as charmer Ron Jenkins.

★ Before finding fame as Purdey in the *New Avengers*, Joanna Lumley played Ken Barlow's girlfriend Elaine Perkins in *Coronation Street*.

★ Shaun Williamson, better known as *EastEnders'* Barry Evans, played the paramedic who attended to Michelle after she was shot in the Queen Vic in 1994.

★ Although to many she will always be Nora Batty, actress Kathy Staff has done the rounds of the soaps. She was Winnie Purves in *Emmerdale*, shopkeeper Vera Hopkins in *Coronation Street*, and Doris Luke in *Crossroads*.

★ Actress Pam St Clement, who plays Pat Evans in *EastEnders*, appeared in *Emmerdale* in 1979, playing a character called Mrs Eckersly.

★ *'Allo 'Allo* star Gordon Kaye also made an early appearance in the Yorkshire Dales. He played a postman.

★ Ross Kemp also spent time in Yorkshire before heading to Walford. In the mid-80s he appeared in *Emmerdale* playing Dolly Skilbeck's long-lost son, Graham Lodsworth.

★ Hollywood heart-throb Russell Crowe appeared in *Neighbours* long before he wowed the world as a *Gladiator*. He played Kenny Larkin back in 1987.

★ Theatre impresario Bill Kenwright appeared in *Coronation Street* before he started putting musicals on the London stage. He played Gordon Clegg, the illegitimate son of Betty Turpin.

CELEBRITIES WHO HAVE APPEARED AS
THEMSELVES IN SOAP OPERAS

Soap operas are now so popular, that many celebrities are more than happy to appear in the shows as themselves. Unfortunately, in some cases their acting proved more wooden than a tree. Don't give up the day job!

★ Michael Parkinson appeared in *Brookside* interviewing Jackie Corkhill and Patricia Farnham on a chat show debating Mandy and Beth Jordache's jail sentence and campaigning against it.

★ Linda Lusardi made a brief appearance in *Hollyoaks* in 1998 when she officially reopened Tony's video shop.

★ Sir Trevor McDonald presented the news broadcast of Prince Charles walking down *Coronation Street*'s famous cobbles during the live fortieth-anniversary episode of the soap.

★ The Pet Shop Boys once turned up in *Neighbours*. They appeared in Ramsey Street to ask where the recording studio was.

★ Ian Botham reopened the Woolpack in *Emmerdale*, after it was severely damaged by the infamous plane crash of 1993. Fellow cricketer Freddie Trueman has also made an appearance.

★ Atomic Kitten's Jenny Frost and Natasha Hamilton made a brief appearance in *Home and Away*, giving directions to cast members who were lost in London.

★ Loyd Grossman and Lily Savage appeared in *Brookside*, attending the opening of Grant's restaurant.

★ Rugby player Martin Offiah got some action when he appeared in *Hollyoaks*. He snogged Maddie at a party. He also played himself in an episode of *Emmerdale*.

★ Eamonn Holmes and Lorraine Kelly turned up in *Brookside* interviewing Penny Crosbie on breakfast television.

★ Television presenter Sarah Greene featured in *Brookside* as a special guest at a charity fashion show.

★★★★★★★★★★★★★★★★★★
CELEBRITY HEIGHTS
★★★★★★★★★★★★★★★★★★★

When I was working in radio, I got to meet many famous people. Whenever my friends asked me what certain celebrities were like, I usually found myself saying, 'They were much smaller than they look on the telly.' This was certainly the case when I met Kylie Minogue and Natalie Imbruglia at the same time. I am 5ft 7in and usually wear 3-inch heels in an attempt to appear taller and slimmer. Standing next to them was like standing next to the Oompa Loompa's in *Charlie and the Chocolate Factory*. I am sure I weighed more than both of them put together!

However, not all celebrities are that small.

Barbara Windsor – 4'10"
Kylie Minogue – 5'0"
Dawn French – 5'0"
Ronnie Corbett – 5'1"
Andrea Corr – 5'1"
Emma Bunton – 5'2"
Jessie Wallace (*EastEnders*' Kat Slater) – 5'2"
Julia Sawalha – 5'3"
Letitia Dean (*EastEnders*' Sharon) – 5'3"
Madonna – 5'4"
JK Rowling – 5'4"
Michael J Fox – 5'4"

Sanjeev Bhaskar (*The Kumars at No 42*) – 5'5"
Victoria Beckham – 5'6"
David Jason – 5'6"
Mick Jagger – 5'7"
Phil Collins – 5'8"
Joanna Lumley – 5'8"
Michael Jackson – 5'9"
Vic Reeves – 5'9"
Naomi Campbell – 5'10"
Graham Norton – 5'10"
George Michael – 5'11"
Nicole Kidman – 5'11"
Sigourney Weaver – 5'11"
Shane Richie – 6'0"
Eva Herzigova – 6'0"
Penny Lancaster – 6'1"
Chris Evans – 6'2"
James Alexandrou (*EastEnders'* Martin Fowler) – 6'2"
Chris Tarrant – 6'2"
John Cusack (star of the film *High Fidelity*) – 6'3"
Jamie Theakston – 6'4"
Sir Steve Redgrave – 6'5"
Tim Robbins – 6'5"
Will Self – 6'6"
Michael Crichton (*Jurassic Park* writer) – 6'10"

★ Actor Paul Newman once challenged the editor of the *New York Post*, Frank Devine, to a $500,000 bet, after an article in the newspaper stated that he was only 5'8" tall. The editor declined to accept the bet. Newman is 5'9".

FAMOUS PEOPLE WITH THINGS
NAMED AFTER THEM

One of the quirks of being famous is that people like to name things after you. This happens especially in your home town. These things could be anything from a flower to a train, a pub or a whole street. Airports are usually only named after people who are already dead, so if someone ever suggests naming one after you – beware – your days could be numbered!

★ Harrison Ford has had an ant named after him. US scientists named the Central American ant, *Peidole harrisonfordi*, to honour the actor's conservation work.

★ Actress Jane Asher, newsreader Anna Ford, Princess Anne and Paul McCartney have all had roses named after them.

★ Film legend Bob Hope has a theatre named after him in Eltham.

★ Singer Tina Turner has a road named after her. Part of State Highway 19 near Nutbush, Tennessee has been called 'Tina Turner Highway'. The road was mentioned in her song 'Nutbush City Limits'.

★ Actress Kate Winslet has also had a street named after her in her home town of Reading. The cul-de-sac of fifty houses is known as Winslet Place.

★ Singer Marti Pellow has a day named after him. In the US state of Tennessee, 9 May is officially Marti Pellow day.

★ Boxer Henry Cooper has a pub named after him in London.

★ Cricketer Fred Trueman also has a pub named after him – The Fiery Fred in Yorkshire.

★ John Lennon has an airport named after him. Liverpool Airport was renamed 'Liverpool John Lennon Airport' when a new terminal was opened in 2001.

★ Legendary Australian rockers AC/DC have had a Spanish street named after them. It is found in the Leganes district of Madrid.

★ Former *EastEnders* actress Tamzin Outhwaite has had a zebra named after her at Marwell Zoo in Hampshire.

★ Film star Sir Michael Caine has had a song named after him. 'Michael Caine' was a hit for Madness in February 1984 and featured a guest appearance by the man himself.

★ Fellow actor Sean Penn also has a song named after him. Lloyd Cole and the Commotions recorded 'Sean Penn Blues'.

★ Monica Lewinsky has had a vacuum cleaner named after her. The American 'Vac-Tron' industrial vacuum cleaner company made the 'Monica II'.

FAMOUS PEOPLE WHO HAVE HAD CHART SUCCESS

Even though they might be famous in another field of show business, such as presenting or acting, many celebrities feel that they have at least one song in them. Others feel they have a whole album, and believe it is their duty to demonstrate to the nation, exactly how vocally talented they are.

Sometimes, against the odds, these records actually do quite well ...

★ Terry Wogan made it into the charts in 1978 with his version of 'The Floral Dance'. The record peaked at number 21.

★ In 1990, *Emmerdale* actress Malandra Burrows released the single 'Just this Side of Love' after her character Kathy sang it on the programme. It got to number 11.

★ Other *Emmerdale* stars made the chart in 1996. The Woolpackers were comprised of characters Terry, Vic, Zak and Lisa. Their line-dancing song 'Hillbilly Rock, Hillbilly Roll' reached number 5 in the charts.

★ Former *Neighbours* star Craig McLachlan, who played Henry Ramsey, reached number 2 in 1990 with his debut single 'Mona'. An album followed and made number 10 in the album charts.

★ Television presenter Keith Chegwin got to number 3 in 1975 as part of the group Kenny, who had a hit with 'The Bump'.

★ In 1977 actor David Soul, who played the blond half of

Starsky and Hutch, went to number 1 with 'Don't Give Up On Us'.

★ Many years before she donned her famous cardigan, *EastEnders*' Wendy Richard was topping the charts. She and Mike Sarne got to number 1 in 1962 with 'Come Outside'.

★ Five years before he entered the *Celebrity Fame Academy*, actor Will Mellor experienced some chart success. His cover of the Leo Sayer classic 'When I Need You' reached number 5 in the charts.

★ Broadcaster and comedy legend Kenny Everett made the top 10 in March 1983 under the guise of his character 'Sid Snot'. The 'Snot Rap' got to number 9.

★ As half of duo 'Pat and Mick', DJ Pat Sharp had a top 10 hit in 1989 with a cover of the Gonzalez song 'I Haven't Stopped Dancing Yet'.

★ Comedian Jasper Carrott spent an amazing fifteen weeks in the chart in 1975. His novelty single 'Funky Moped' peaked at number 5.

★ In 1986, *Heartbeat* and *In Deep* star Nick Berry topped the charts with 'Every Loser Wins', a song that originally featured in an *EastEnders* storyline, where Nick was playing Simon Wicks. Six years later he was back at number 1 with another television-related tune, this time the title track to the 60s police series *Heartbeat*.

★ Another Albert Square resident, Anita Dobson, who played Angie Watts, made the top 10 in 1986 with a vocal version of the *EastEnders* theme tune. 'Anyone Can Fall In Love' reached number 4 in the charts. In 1988 the tune was transformed once again. This time it became a hymn called 'Glory Be', which was performed on the BBC's *Songs of Praise* programme.

★ Anita's screen daughter Sharon, actress Letitia Dean, just failed to make the top 10 the same year with another song that had featured in the soap. 'Something Outta Nothing', which she performed with fellow *EastEnder* Paul J Medford (who played Kelvin), made it to number 12.

★ Sophie Lawrence, who played Diane Butcher in *EastEnders*, joined the ranks of the 'soapstars-turned-wannabe-popstars' when she released a cover of Donna Summer's 'Love's Unkind' in 1991. It peaked at number 21.

★ Sophie's screen brother Ricky, actor Sid Owen, made his own bid for chart success in 2000. His cover of Sugar Minott's 'Good Thing Going' got to number 14, but a follow-up single failed to make a big impact.

★ Comedian Billy Connolly topped the charts in 1975 with 'DIVORCE'. He was back in the top 40 ten years later with the theme tune to the children's series *Supergran*.

★ Footballer Paul Gascoigne recorded his own unique version of the Lindisfarne classic 'Fog on the Tyne' in November 1990, and made it to number 2 in the charts.

★ Fellow footballer Kevin Keegan was 'Head over Heels in Love' in June 1979. Despite his horrendous perm, the song reached number 31.

★ Equally bad haircuts were seen on soccer stars Glenn Hoddle and Chris Waddle when they performed their single 'Diamond Lights' on *Top of the Pops* in 1987. Their voices were weak and they couldn't dance at all, but the song got to number 12.

★ Another sportsman, boxer Frank Bruno, had a fight on his hands when he joined the race for the Christmas number 1 in 1995. He didn't make it to the top of the charts, but his version of 'Eye of the Tiger' did get to number 28.

★ Actor Bernard Cribbins, the voice of *The Wombles*, and more recently seen as Wally Bannister in *Coronation Street*, had two top-10 hits in 1962 with the novelty records 'Right Said Fred' and 'Hole in The Ground'.

★ Actor Dennis Waterman had a number 3 hit in 1980 with 'I Could Be so Good for You', the theme tune to the series *Minder* in which he starred. Waterman was back in the charts in December 1983, sharing the stage with his *Minder* co-star George Cole on the song 'What are We Gonna get Her Indoors?'

★ Before finding fame in Hollywood, Catherine Zeta Jones tried to make it big in the charts. 'For All Time' reached number 36 in September 1992, while a recording of the classic 'True Love Ways' with David Essex in November 1994 peaked at 38.

★ David Grant may now be recognised as voice-coach to the stars, following his appearance on *Pop Idol*. During the 80s however, he had six top-40 hits, peaking at number 5 in 1985 with 'Could it Be I'm Falling in Love', in which he performed a duet with Jaki Graham.

★ Comedian and former *EastEnder* Mike Reid got to number 10 in 1975 with 'The Ugly Duckling'. A quarter of a century later his version of 'The More I See You', which he performed with fellow *EastEnder* Barbara Windsor, failed to do so well; it only reached number 46.

★ Fellow comedian Alexei Sayle had a hit in 1984 with the catchily titled 'Ullo, John, Got a New Motor'. It reached number 15 in the charts.

AND THOSE WHO TRIED BUT WERE
NEVER TOP OF THE POPS

For every Nick Berry single that flies off the shelf and becomes a number one, there are at least a dozen other soap stars and celebrity wannabes who never make the grade – or even the top 40.

Here are some of the worse offenders.

★ Oscar-winning actor Anthony Hopkins spent one week in the charts in 1986 with the song 'Distant Star'. It peaked at a lowly 75.

★ Supermodel Naomi Campbell may be top of the pops when it comes to the catwalk, but her attempts at a recording career were far from successful. 'Love and Tears' only reached number 40 in September 1994.

★ Television presenter Dani Behr made a bid for chart success while still a teenager, as part of the girl group Faith, Hope and Charity. Unfortunately their single 'Battle of the Sexes' was not the start of great things. It peaked at 53.

★ Comedian Steve Coogan tried to make it into the top 40 in 1996, disguised as Latin lothario Tony Ferrino. His double A-side 'Help Yourself/Bigamy at Christmas' made it to number 42.

★ *Miami Vice* heart-throb Don Johnson attempted to capitalise on his worldwide fame by releasing the single 'Heartbeat' in 1986. The women of Britain may have fancied him, but they didn't fancy his singing much – it got to number 46.

★ The public may have laughed at Maureen Rees's motoring skills when she appeared in *Driving School*, but they were certainly not amused by her singing. Her 1997 version of 'Driving in My Car' peaked at 49.

★ In 2002, war correspondent and former independent MP Martin Bell became a rap star. He sang 'in a Rex Harrison style' on a hip-hop single called 'Media Junkies'.

★ Radio 2 presenter Steve Wright released three records during the early 80s. His 1982 offering 'I'm Alright', which he performed with the Afternoon Boys, managed to reach number 40 and remain in the charts for six weeks. However his 1983 release 'Get Some Therapy' spent only one week at number 75, while his 1984 recording of 'The Gay Cavalieros' peaked only slightly higher at 61. He decided not to give up the day job.

★ Not content with scoring lots of goals for Arsenal, Ian Wright ventured into the music world in 1993. He proved to be less successful in the studio than he was on the pitch – 'Do the Right Thing' only reached number 43.

★ Loyd Grossman once made a pop record under the name 'Jet Bronx and the Forbidden'. His song 'Ain't Doin' Nothin' got to number 49 in 1977.

★ In 2000, actor Kevin Kennedy, better known as *Coronation Street*'s Curly Watts, released the single 'Bulldog Nation'. It managed to sell only 24,000 copies and entered the charts at 51.

★ Before she was wowing West End audiences, Denise van Outen was just another pop hopeful, as one half of a duo called Those Two Girls. Unfortunately being hopeful was not enough to bring success.

★ In the early 1980s, comedian Ricky Gervais was part of a New Romantic synthesizer group called 'Seona Dancing'. The band reached number 116 and 70 in the chart with their first two releases before being dropped by their record company.

★ *Coronation Street*'s Audrey Roberts, actress Sue Nicholls, had a top-20 hit in 1968 with 'Where Will You Be'. She was asked to record the track after performing it on *Crossroads*. It entered the charts at number 17.

★ *EastEnders*' Bianca and Ricky, Sid Owen and Patsy Palmer, were doing it for 'charidee', when they released the single 'Better Believe It' in 1995. Unfortunately the public couldn't believe how bad it was, and the single only spent one week in the charts at number 60.

★ Actor Albert Finney released *The Albert Finney Album* in 1977. A career in music did not follow.

★ Jim Davidson may be a success as a comedian, but singing was obviously not a strong point. His Christmas offering in 1980, a version of 'White Christmas', only made it to number 52.

★ Actor Robert Downey Jnr did even worse with his 1993 release 'Smile'. It spent only one week in the charts, appearing at number 68.

★ Although she never made it on to *Top of the Pops*, when Davina McCall was trying to break into pop music her demo tape was produced by Eric Clapton.

★ *Heartbeat* co-star Nick Berry may have topped the charts, but Tricia Penrose, who played barmaid Geena, struggled to make it in at all. Her 1996 release 'Where Did the Love Go' only reached number 71.

★ She may have been royalty, but Princess Stephanie of Monaco's foray into pop with the 1986 single 'Live Your Life' didn't bring her any gold or platinum discs.

★ In the early 90s *EastEnders* actress Michelle Collins recorded a cover of the Temptations classic 'Get Ready'. Musical success did not follow, so she returned to Albert Square.

★ Radio presenters Bruno Brookes and Liz Kershaw released a version of 'It Takes Two, Baby' in 1989. The song only reached number 53 in the charts, but undeterred they released a second single the year after. 'Let's Dance' did even worse, peaking at 54.

★ *Coronation Street's* Maxine Peacock, actress Tracy Shaw, attempted an assault on the charts in 1998 with a cover of Lonnie Gordon's 'Happenin' All Over Again'. It failed to get into the top 40, peaking at number 46.

★ He may have introduced many number ones as a DJ, but Tony Blackburn only managed to scrape into the top 50 during the late 1960s with the singles 'So Much Love' and 'It's Only Love'.

★ Uri Geller released a solo album entitled *Uri Geller* in 1975.

★ *Absolutely Fabulous* star June Whitfield once had a record banned by the BBC. She recorded a spoof version of 'Je T'aime' with Frankie Howerd, but BBC executives decided that the ironic heavy breathing was too hot for broadcast.

★ Russell Crowe has made several attempts at a music career, at one time playing in a band called 'Roman Antix' under the name Russ Le Roc. His first single was entitled 'I Want to Be Like Marlon Brando'.

★ Musical lyricist Sir Tim Rice was a member of the pop group The Aardvarks from 1961–63, and also sang with the equally unsuccessful Whang and the Cheviots.

★ *Coronation Street* actress Barbara Knox, who plays Rita Sullivan, recorded an album in the early 70s entitled *On the Street Where I Live*.

CELEBRITY FIRSTS

Neil Armstrong may be known around the globe for walking on the moon, but he is not the only person to enter the record books for being the first person to do something. Many famous people have their own place in history for the most unlikely reasons.

★ Noel Edmonds hosted the UK's first ever National Lottery show.

★ While performing together during the early 1990s, Rob Newman and David Baddiel became the first comedians ever to perform at Wembley Arena.

★ Sir Trevor McDonald was the first black male newsreader on British television, when he appeared on ITN in 1973. Moira Stuart was the first black female newsreader when she first appeared in 1981.

★ Sir Trevor was also the first British broadcaster to interview Nelson Mandela on his release from prison and the first to interview Saddam Hussein after his invasion of Kuwait in 1990.

★ Sidney Poitier was the first black leading actor to win an Oscar. He picked up the statue for his role in the 1963 film *Lillies of the Field*.

★ It wasn't until 2002 that Halle Berry became the first black leading actress to win an Oscar. She took the title for her performance in *Monster's Ball*.

★ Elizabeth Taylor was the first Hollywood star to receive a million dollars for a single film – *Cleopatra* in 1963.

★ Meanwhile Julia Roberts became the first woman to earn $20 million, for the film *Erin Brockovich*.

★ Kate Adie was the first woman news reporter on British television to broadcast live from a combat situation when she covered the SAS storming of the Iranian Embassy in London in 1980.

★ *Countdown* presenter Richard Whiteley was the first person to appear on screen on Channel 4, when it launched in November 1982.

★ Cindy Crawford was the first modern supermodel to pose for *Playboy*.

★ Annie Nightingale was the first female DJ on Radio 1.

★ It took another nineteen years before *GMTV* correspondent Jakki Brambles became the first female DJ to be given a daytime slot on Radio 1.

★ Britney Spears was the first solo artist ever to have a number one album and single on the American *Billboard* charts at the same time with a debut (*Baby, One More Time*).

★ James Dean was the first actor to be nominated for an Oscar posthumously in 1956. Dean was killed in a car accident six months earlier, only a few days after he completed filming on *Giant*, the film for which he received his nomination. (He didn't win the Oscar, however – it went to Yul Brynner for his performance in *The King and I*.)

★ Marianne Faithful was the first actress to utter the F-word in a film. It was in *I'll Never Forget Whatsisname* in 1966.

★ Claudia Schiffer was the first model to feature on the cover of *Rolling Stone* magazine.

★ *Coronation Street* actor Johnny Briggs (Mike Baldwin) starred in Britain's first X-rated film. The film was *Cosh Boy*.

CELEBRITY FOOTBALL FANS

Football is said to be the new rock'n'roll, so it's no surprise that many celebrities are keen to attach themselves to certain soccer teams.

But who is supporting who when the whistle blows at three o'clock on a Saturday afternoon?

★ Clive Anderson, *Jonathan Creek* actor Alan Davies, singing sisters Nicole and Natalie Appleton and former boxer Nigel Benn all support Arsenal.

★ Canadian rocker Bryan Adams, Blur's Damon Albarn, Sir Michael Caine and comedian David Baddiel are all fans of Chelsea.

★ Chris de Burgh, Les Dennis, *Red Dwarf* star Craig Charles and Cilla Black support Liverpool.

★ Actors Hugh Grant and Keith Allen are Fulham supporters.

★ *Smack the Pony*'s Fiona Allen, comedian Peter Kay and radio presenter Emma Forbes support Bolton Wanderers.

★ Sir David Frost, Craig David and *They Think it's All Over* star David Gower are Southampton supporters.

★ Comedian Brian Conley and Elton John are Watford fans.

★ Steve Coogan, broadcaster Terry Christian, Radio 1 DJ Edith Bowman, Zoë Ball and Irish premier Bertie Aherne all support Manchester United.

★ *Men Behaving Badly* star Neil Morrissey, and comedians Eddie Izzard, Jo Brand and Ronnie Corbett are supporters of Crystal Palace.

★ Famous West Bromwich Albion supporters include Frank Skinner, Eric Clapton and *Working Lunch* presenter Adrian Chiles.

★ England cricket captain Nassar Hussain, Mel B, Chinese chef Ken Hom and *Fat Friends* actress Gaynor Faye are Leeds United supporters.

★ Norman Cook and television presenter Jamie Theakston both support Brighton and Hove Albion. So does Des Lynam.

★ Ozzy Osbourne, former *Professional* Martin Shaw, Radio 1 DJ Emma B and Tory leader Iain Duncan Smith are all fans of Aston Villa.

★ Actor Kenneth Branagh, Phil Collins, heart-throb Jude Law, *The Fast Show's* Paul Whitehouse and film critic Barry Norman all support Tottenham Hotspur.

★ Famous Everton fans include Sir Paul McCartney and Atomic Kitten's Liz McClarnon.

★ *EastEnders* actor Adam Woodyatt, comedian Arthur Smith and *RI:SE* presenter Mel Giedroyc, half of Mel and Sue, are Wimbledon supporters.

★ Bob Mortimer, *Ballykissangel* star Stephen Tompkinson, and singer Chris Rea are all fans of Middlesbrough.

★ Ant and Dec, Prime Minister Tony Blair, actor Robson Green and former boxer Chris Eubank support Newcastle.

★ Nick Berry, former *EastEnder* Todd Carty (Mark Fowler), comedian Phill Jupitus and boxer Lennox Lewis are West Ham fans.

CELEBRITY DEATHS

This last selection features some famous people whose manner of death was as much a part of the news story as their passing away. They may be gone, but they are certainly not forgotten.

★ Comedian and magician Tommy Cooper died on stage in 1984. He was appearing in *Live from Her Majesty's*, wearing his famous red fez, when he suffered a fatal heart attack. Some viewers at the time believed his collapse was part of his act.

★ Fellow comedian Eric Morecambe collapsed as he came off stage in Tewkesbury in May 1984, and died a few hours later, after also suffering from a heart attack. His comedy partner Ernie Wise said at the time, 'It's the saddest day of my life ... I feel like I've lost a limb, I have been robbed of a partner and brother, there is a cold draught down one side of me where Eric should be.'

★ In December 2000 singer Kirsty MacColl died in a boating accident in Cozumel, Mexico, where she was holidaying with her two sons. The accident happened when a speedboat, which was travelling illegally in an area reserved for swimmers, hit Kirsty, a keen diver. Her two children were with her in the water at the time.

★ In 1997 the fashion designer Gianni Versace was murdered on the steps of his Miami home. He had left his beach mansion to buy some magazines, when Andrew Cunanan, a serial killer who the FBI had been hunting across America for the previous month, shot him three times at close range.

★ In 1993 actor River Phoenix died from a lethal cocktail of cocaine, heroin, Valium, ephedrine and marijuana, after collapsing at Johnny Depp's club The Viper Room in Los Angeles. He was just 23 years old. Shocked fans were left puzzled, as the star of *Stand By Me* had always said he was opposed to the use of drugs.

★ On 4 April 1994, Nirvana front man Kurt Cobain was found dead in his own home. The 27-year-old had shot himself in the mouth. He had written a suicide note, warning his daughter not to be like him. Some have said that the note was really his resignation and that he was murdered; however, his diaries later revealed that he had bought a gun with which to shoot himself two years before his death, as he wanted to escape a painful stomach illness.

★ INXS singer Michael Hutchence was found dead in a Sydney hotel room in November 1997, aged 37. A New South Wales coroner recorded his death as suicide by hanging, but many continue to believe Hutchence had been involved in an accidentally fatal sex act.

★ Less than three years after Hutchence's death, his partner, television presenter Paula Yates, died at her home in London aged forty. The inquest found her death had been caused by nondependent use of drugs, after taking heroin. She had been devastated by the death of Hutchence, and had spent time in hospital suffering from depression. However, her friends say that she would never have deliberately ended her own life, because of her devotion to her children.

★ In 1996 actress Margaux Hemingway committed suicide by overdosing on sedatives. She was the fifth person in her family to take their own life. Her grandfather, the famous writer Ernest Hemingway, shot himself in 1961.

★ Soul legend Marvin Gaye was shot dead by his father, the day before his 45th birthday on 1 April 1984, following a violent disagreement. The previous month Gaye had announced to relatives that he had intended to take his own life, and once had a gun forcibly removed from his hand. Friends had become increasingly concerned about his mental state and his growing dependence on drugs.

★ In 1973, at the age of 32, martial arts star Bruce Lee died in Hong Kong from an apparent cerebral oedema – a swelling of the brain – several hours after taking a prescribed painkiller. Doctors declared the death of Bruce Lee was 'death by misadventure', and said that he had experienced a bad reaction to the aspirin within the painkiller. Others continue to speculate as to whether his death was the result of a family curse or a Triad killing.

★ Bruce Lee's son, Brandon Lee, was also the victim of an untimely death, after being fatally wounded on the set of his film *The Crow*. While filming one scene, a tip from a 'dummy round' (a prop bullet which has no gunpowder), which had got stuck in the gun, was ejected from the barrel when a blank cartridge was fired, and got lodged in his spine after penetrating his abdomen. His death came just seventeen days before he was to be married to his fiancée, Eliza Hutton.

★ In 1985 Hollywood actor Rock Hudson died of AIDS. He was the first major public figure to admit that he had the disease.

★ In 2001 Grammy-nominated R&B singer Aaliyah was among nine people killed when their plane crashed and burst into flames shortly after taking off in the Bahamas. An autopsy performed on the pilot of the plane, who was also killed in the crash, found cocaine in his urine and alcohol in his stomach.

★ Karen Carpenter died on 4 February 1983 of heart failure caused by chronic anorexia nervosa, at the age of 32. She had battled with the disorder since 1975. She fought to overcome it during the last two years of her life, but her body was too weak, following the persistent use of laxatives and thyroid pills.

★ In 1967 'Reet Petite' singer Jackie Wilson collapsed on stage as he suffered a stroke and a heart attack. He never regained consciousness and died eight years later.

★ On 5 August 1962 film legend Marilyn Monroe was found nude and lying face down on her bed. The official verdict is that she died from acute barbiturate poisoning, after overdosing on the drugs Nembutal and chloral hydrate, which were both prescribed for insomnia. How this overdose came about, however, is the subject of much controversy. While many see it as suicide, other theorists have suggested it was either a self-administered accidental overdose, an accidental overdose administered by someone else, or murder. The conspiracy theory is strengthened by the fact that the scene of death appeared to have been tampered with, important tissue samples from the autopsy mysteriously disappeared, and the knowledge that she had an affair with President John F Kennedy.

BIBLIOGRAPHY

Books

The Virgin Book of Film Records, Phil Swern and Toby Rowan, Virgin (1999)

Who's Really Who, Compton Miller, Harden's Books (1997)

Who's Who on Television, ITV books (1988)

30 Years of Emmerdale, Lance Parkin, Granada (2002)

Pop Idol: The official story of the ITV Series, Sian Solanas, Carlton (2002)

Emmerdale: Real Soap, Deborah Tilley, Generation Productions (2001)

Opening Shots, Damien Bona, Workman (1994)

Brat Pack Confidential, Andrew Pulver and Steven Paul Davies, BT Batsford (2000)

Hollyoaks:The Official Companion, Matthew Evans, Channel 4 Books (2002)

The Celebrity Lists Book, Mitchell Symons, Andre Deutsch (1998)

The New and Revised Guinness Who's Who of Soap Operas, Anthony Haward, Guinness (1995)

Cuty TV, The Comedies, Jon E. Lewis and Penny Stempel, Pavilion (1998)

Who's Who on Radio, Sheila Tracy, World's Work Ltd (1983)

Where are they Now, Andy Pringle, Two Heads Publishing (1997)

Journolists, John Koski and Mitchell Symons, Chapmans (1992)

Box of Delights, Hilary Kingsley and Geoff Tibballs, MacMillan (1989)

The Guinness Book of TV Facts and Feats, Kenneth Passingham, Guinness (1984)

On Second Thoughts, Gary Belsky, Michael O'Mara (1999)

Top Ten: The Irreverent Guide to Music, Alex Ogg, Channel 4 books (2001)

The Book of Bizarre Football, Graham Sharpe, Robson Books (2000)

Madonna, Andrew Morton, Michael O'Mara (2001)

Voice of an Angel, Charlotte Church, Little, Brown (2001)

Bruce: The Autobiography, Pan Books (2001)

Is It Me? Terry Wogan: The Autobiography, Terry Wogan, BBC Books (2000)

Nicole Kidman: The Biography, Tim Ewbank and Stafford Hildred, Headline (2002)

Liam Neeson, The First Biography, Ingrid Millar, Hodder and Stoughton (1995)

J K Rowling: A Biography, Sean Smith, Michael O'Mara (2001)

Judi Dench: With a Crack in Her Voice, John Miller, Weidenfeld and Nicolson (1997)

Fighting Talk: The Biography of John Prescott, Colin Brown, Simon and Schuster (1997)

Jamie Oliver: The Biography, Stafford Hildred and Tim Ewbank, John Blake Publishing (2001)

The Richard and Judy Story, Carole Malone, Virgin (1996)

Dale: My Story, Dale Winton, Century Books (2002)

Frank Skinner, Frank Skinner, Century Books (2001)

Beckham: My World, David Beckham, Hodder and Stoughton (2000)

Together, Nicole and Natalie Appleton, Michael Joseph (2002)

Film Stars, Bob McCabe, HarperCollins (1999)

The Guinness Book of British Hit Singles 15th Edition, Guinness

Officially Osbourne, Todd Gold, Simon and Schuster (2002)

Internet

BBCi / www.channel4.com / www.thisdayinmusic.com / www.ananova.com

Newspapers

Express / Daily Mail / Sun / Mirror / Guardian / Daily Telegraph / Sunday Telegraph / The Times / Mail on Sunday / Sunday Express / Observer / Independent on Sunday / The Sunday Times